Spy

The No-Good Pup

Spy
The No-Good Pup

JOYCE STRANGER

Illustrated by Terry Riley

J.M.Dent & Sons Ltd · London

First published in Great Britain in 1989

Printed in Great Britain at
The Bath Press, Avon
for J.M.Dent & Sons Ltd
91 Clapham High Street
London SW4 7TA

British Cataloguing-in-Publication Data

Stranger, Joyce
Spy, the no good pup
I. Title II. Riley, Terry
823' .914

ISBN 0-460-07043-6

To Janus (1971–1984) and Puma (1972–1981)
who would have been much better trained
if I had known then what I know now

ONE

THE BLACK and white pup had been bred on one of the oldest farms in Wales. It was a tiny building, hidden under the hill. Clustering trees protected it from the savage storms that drove down the mountain.

He was born in the Spring when the lambs were dancing in fields where new grass sprang to life; when the vixen hid her cubs under the rocky crag that shielded her den from rain and sun; when soft feathered birds sat on their nests, sheltering fragile shelled eggs, waiting for the telltale cheeps, and the cracking of the protective cover that meant new life.

He was born knowing nothing of the world he was to

inherit. His first sight, when his eyes opened, would be of wooden walls, deep straw, and a black head with bright eyes watching him, as his mother nosed him and told him, with her body, how a pup should behave.

The first days of Spring had been warm; days of sunshine, and golden flowers, and bright birds singing. The old farmer had whistled as he worked, remembering his youth as the heat comforted bones that often protested when the weather turned wet or cold.

The litter was expected, was longed for, but it was not due for another week. Tom could go to bed and sleep in peace, knowing that all was well. He stroked his bitch, and closed the door on her, making sure she was safe.

Though she was his companion, his friend, his need, for he could never work the sheep without her, she was not allowed in the house. The yard and the shed was the place for a dog. Only in deepest snow, or when the troughs were solid with ice and the yard a skating rink, did she come in to sleep in the concrete floored lean-to beyond the old kitchen.

The pup was born on a night of wind and driving rain, rain that seeped under the cracks of the old shed, rain that kept old Tom indoors, unaware that his bitch had come early to whelping. The bitch whimpered, wanting comforting hands on her body, her master's presence beside her, but the creaking branches of the old trees drowned her cries. The gale strengthened and great gusts tore at the ageing wood, the boughs bent to the ground, or cracked off, the sound savage on the air, and there was no hope that Tom would hear her.

Mel knew all about pups. This was her fourth litter, and she was wise and experienced, needing no man to show her what had to be done. Her master could not come, so she resigned herself to bearing the pups alone.

As each of the mites was born, she licked away the birth coverings, leaving the puppy clean, and nudged it into her side to feed.

Five times she brought a tiny body to her front paws. Five times she nudged and licked and watched, and felt the overpowering maternal surge of love for these, her puppies.

The sixth time was different. The pup was slow to come, and she was weary. The birth pains were remorseless, telling her that she must not give up. Now, and now and now.

At last the pup was free of her, but he lay, almost lifeless, nearly defeated by the long struggle that had brought him into a cold dark world. Mel also lay quiet, feeling too exhausted to care for this, her last-born.

Outside, the wind wailed, whipping round the corners, pushing intrusive invisible fingers into the straw that lined her bed. It chilled her, and wearily, painfully, she dragged herself up, moving each pup, one by one to the deeper straw at the back of the shed, out of reach of the creeping draught.

She moved her last-born, easing him against her as she settled, her back to the crack under the door, shielding her family.

She had pulled the covering from his nose, nibbling with gentle teeth, so that he could breathe. But she sensed now that this pup was near to death. She began to lick him. Then she took him in her jaws and shook him, as though she were killing a rat. The swift movement brought life to his lungs so that he gasped and whimpered, a forlorn cry that impelled his mother to greater efforts.

The busy tongue licked on. The pup moved his paws, moved his ears, and nuzzled against her. She felt his breath on her nose, and pushed him hard against the overflowing teat. At last he began to suck. She watched him, brown eyes intent. She had worked on him for nearly ten minutes, had fought to save him, and the ferocity of her love for this pup which had nearly escaped her brought her tongue into play again, caressing him, nursing him, almost forgetting that the other five had need of her ministrations too.

She relaxed at last, sure that everything was well with all six of her babies, and lay, dreaming, resting, aware of the pressure of the small bodies against her, of their sucking mouths, of their tiny paws, of the new life that had come to join her in the long hours of the night. She nosed them, savouring the new-born smell of them, a smell that reminded her of her other pups, long gone now, but that told her exactly what she had to do.

She slept.

Morning brought calm; and showed destruction. Four of the sheltering trees had fallen in the night. Old Tom looked in dismay at the chaos surrounding his home. More work; the daily work was hard enough and he had been alone since his wife had died. There were sheep in the fields, needing his attention, and new lambs likely to be born among them. There was enough for a man to do without God throwing his storms at him.

There was a tangle of branches round the shed, but none of the heavy trunks had harmed the place. Tom clambered among the leaves, and pushed the door open.

He called.

"Mel, girl, Mel!"

She did not come.

Tom opened the door wider, letting in sunshine that brightened the straw and shone on the wriggling pups that struggled to feed. The old man stared. Over a week early, and he not there to help her. He had been idle in his bed while she was enduring the long agony in the dark night, and no food to comfort her when it was done. Nor his hand on her head to praise her for her efforts.

Guilt needled him, and he knelt to look at the litter, to run his hands over her body, to make sure all was well. She greeted him with a licked face.

She was his daytime companion, his confidante, his only real friend now that the children were grown and gone: young Tom to Australia and little Rhian, who had been so pretty, to marry a man who took her to faraway California. She sent Tom long letters, and pictures of his grandchildren, now well grown, but it was not the same as having your own about you and close, as his own brothers and sisters had been close, long ago. Now, he was the only one left.

"I should not have gone to bed and left you here alone," he told the bitch. She, always forgiving, licked his hand, and watched as he took each pup and examined it carefully, looking for deformities.

He sighed with relief. All were fine strong beautiful little pups. Mel, watching him intently, saw the well-known smile, and pushed her body against him, asking for his praise. This he never stinted, and now, looking down at the healthy pups, knowing nothing of the battle she had fought with death in the night, he smiled again.

Birth, to him, was a recurring triumph, a miracle that where the night before there had been only one animal he now had seven. Six more small creatures to make their mark in the world. Mel had six pups every time, almost as if she were programmed to do so.

There were eighteen of her pups already working on farms around the county. Two were making their mark in sheepdog trials. The rest were shepherds' dogs, as necessary to the men as their right arms, and sometimes of far more use as they reached sheep that no man could reach, and found them when they were buried in snow, or lost on the hills in the mists that came down so fast that they hid everything before a man had time to sneeze.

Life! It was God's gift to mankind. His only gift. Everything else a man had to find for himself. Tom whistled as he walked across the yard. He had work to do, and if the bitch was too busy with her pups, he would have to do it alone. Mel sat, her pups struggling to feed, and watched him, knowing that he needed her. She was torn between her duty and mother love.

Tom turned back to look again at the family. This once, the sheep could wait. Sunlight dappled the cobbles. A blue morning and a rain-washed sky, clean and innocent. It was hard to believe that the night before the wind had savaged the trees, scarring the mountainside by tearing lumps of rock from their places, hurling them down the slopes.

The farm was safe. Tom was always afraid of mountain slips, which might destroy the fields where his sheep grazed. He looked around him at the work that grew more arduous as the years robbed him of his strength. He had neglected his duty but his dog was safe, and no harm had come to her through leaving her to whelp alone. He went back to her, thanking God for helping her when her master had failed her.

He knelt, awkwardly, in the straw, rheumaticky knees protesting.

Three little bitches and three little dogs, and one of the dogs with the patterning of his father. Tom did not know he was looking at the last-born, the pup that had nearly died. Now he was as sturdy as the rest, a bigger pup than the others, pushing against his sister, and whimpering more loudly than any when his mother stood to go outside and drink eagerly from a large puddle.

Inside, the abandoned pups whiffled at the loss of milk and warmth and struggled in the straw, trying to suck from one another. Small mouths sought frenziedly, blind heads nosed the air, and the seeking lips fastened on paw or tail or ear, and pulled desperately, and whimpered again when no milk came.

The sheep must wait. Tom went indoors, and warmed a pan of gruel that he had intended for his own breakfast. The bitch needed food. He should not have left her on her own. Yet how could he know that she would whelp early? He watched her gulp eagerly, and then run back to her pups, settling herself in among them, nosing each one, as if counting heads.

Six strong puppies. The bitches were already spoken for. Three farmers wanted to breed, and Tom's stock was famous. Two dogs to sell, and the third he would train himself, and start on its long career. He had a debt to pay to young Sam down the valley, who came every day to check on his neighbour, and helped him around the farm.

Sam, who came from over the border, longed to take part in sheepdog trials. He had his own dog, but not well trained and not well bred; a rough dog that had no finesse and little loyalty. A tough dog that at the scent of a bitch left his master's side and the sheep he was herding and only returned when he was ready.

Sam forgave him because Trip had a merry way with him, a laughing mouth and a glint in his eyes, as if he were mocking at mere humans. He was no lapdog, ready to lick a hand. He was a boss dog, his own dog, ready to work if he chose and was in the mood, but a demon to handle if he felt contrary. Sam was not yet a good enough dogman to get the best from the dog. Trip knew it, and mocked his master when he felt the need.

The biggest pup was destined for Sam.

TWO

Meanwhile, not twelve hours old and as yet blind and deaf, the pup slept, and fed, and crept into the straw, and pushed against his mother and his litter mates, starting on the long process of growing to maturity.

Sam, aware of storm damage, came early that day. He was shown his pup. Mel bared her teeth at him. He smiled, and patted her on the head.

"I won't touch him yet, I promise," he told her, and old Tom nodded his head, satisfied. Sam would make a good dogman, one day. He needed taking in hand. He was a city man, born in Birmingham, knowing nothing of the countryside, but there had been no work for him there. He had rented the little small-holding down the valley, and worked hard, making enough money to rent more fields, and then, when his father died and left him a small inheritance, he had bought the buildings and the land and settled down.

Dark clouds drifted over the soft blue sky. Rain threatened. The men worked to clear the yard of fallen trees. Tom thought of the son who had left his side. He would have liked to teach him how to farm. Instead, he was teaching another man's son.

Life did strange things to people. Not like the old days, when families grew up together and stayed together and you married the lass next door and set up in your father's home. The whole family worked the farm.

Now his son was a factory owner in a country Tom had never seen and his daughter was married to a lawyer in yet another faraway land. Sam's father had thought his son a fool for renting a small run-down farm in a mountain valley where the winds seared the crops and nothing grew except scrub and scrawny trees and a few spindly vegetables, and sheep.

Sam whistled as he worked. Excitement mastered him. A new pup. A new beginning. A new future. He couldn't wait for it to grow up.

Tom, hearing him, grinned to himself. He had not forgotten the feeling. Nobody could tell yet how those small animals would turn out, but there was always the hope that this one was the world beater, the dog to beat all dogs.

His mind went back to the old days, when he was well known for his success at sheepdog trials. His constant rival was Jacko Leigh. No, not Leigh. He was Max Leigh's father, and Max had married a man named Leigh.

Memory was a traitor at times. The surname was on

the tip of his tongue and he couldn't remember it. He did remember Jacko and the battles they had, each with his own dog, beating the other by only one or two points. Now Tom was first and now Jacko. It all depended on the sheep.

Max was a winner herself these days. Very few women entered sheepdog trials, but Max and her daughter, Charlie, were always competing. Maxina and Charlotte. He knew them as neighbours, but not as friends.

There was work to do.

"Daydreaming, Tom?" Sam called across the yard. The old man had been standing at the shed door, looking down on the litter for so long that the younger man wondered if something was wrong.

"Remembering," Tom said. "Back when I was working Nim. He was a terrific dog. Those were good days. Pity age betrays you. I'm not as young as I was."

Sam laughed.

"Nor am I and perhaps it's as well. You'd have called me a tearaway ten years ago, when I had a motor bike and drove round the country with my pals. We never did any harm, but we were a noisy lot."

"Young men are like teenage pups," Tom said. He laughed again. "I remember when Mary was alive. She had a fancy for tubs of marigolds all round the yard to pretty it up, and I planted four of them on her birthday. Took hours. Nim raced round the yard at top speed that evening and took every blessed flower out of the tubs. I was mad with the dog, but Mary just laughed and put them all back again."

Sam grinned at the thought of the busy pup, and went on whistling. The day was drab with a drizzle of rain but nothing could damp his spirits. A new puppy of his own, to bring up properly this time.

The soft notes reassured the bitch, who left her pups briefly now and again to come and inspect the yard, to watch the men, and to wait, hopefully, for Tom to remember that now she had pups to feed she was very hungry.

Tom did remember at eleven when the men went into the kitchen for coffee and a bite to eat. He made thick sandwiches of bread and cheese. Cutting wood sharpened the appetite. He broke bread into a bowl and covered it with milk from the dairy cow he kept for his own needs.

Mel barked at him from the open doorway, asking him to hurry. She was so empty that she felt as if she had never eaten in her life before, and the pups, she knew, needed milk. Hurry, hurry, hurry, said her impatient voice. She danced on four paws in a tight circle, barking shrilly because her master was so slow and the gnawing ache inside her so urgent.

Sam cut a large slice of bread and threw it to her. She caught it and gnawed it hungrily.

"They're all alike when they've pups," Tom said, adding gravy to the mash of meat and chopped raw cabbage and the vitamin powder the vet had given him for Mel. He watched her wolf her food, delighting in her, and when she came to him briefly, patted her head.

"You're a grand lass," he said. "Go and feed those pups and make them good and strong for us."

She was impatient to get back to her family. She ran to the shed, to make sure nothing had harmed her pups in her absence. She counted heads. When Sam looked in again, she gave him only a token growl as he did not come near, and he watched for a moment as the busy mouths sucked at her.

His pup. His first pup. He had bought Trip as an adult dog, another man's dog. The shepherd at the far end of the village had hated the animal. Always disobedient, needing a strong hand all the time, an unrewarding dog, sold cheap to a newcomer who knew no better. No other man would have bought Trip.

There was, between man and a dog, a grudging affection; the dog for the man who gave him a roof at night, and shelter from the rain and wind and snow; and fed him. Sam was amused by an independent character that would not brook discipline, but would sometimes work with a will, giving his master a rare taste of the satisfaction that came to those who owned a biddable dog.

Sam was a young man, in his late twenties. Old enough to have learned sense but not yet experienced enough to train a dog with skill. Tom, just over seventy, had lost some of his strength, but none of his knowledge. His grey hair was sparse, close against his head, his beard white. But blue eyes laughed at the world still and he found pleasure in many little things.

Pleasure in the sun patterning the mountains, so that their shapes changed and changed again from hour to hour. He was lost when he went to the flat lands, where only trees broke the skyline. He was born under the shadow of the hills and he needed the giant shapes that reared against the sky. He loved water; the run and ripple and race of clear streams over rounded boulders; the flash and flirt of light on the pouring cascades that leaped from the high rocks above him.

He often stopped work to watch the wide-spread wings of the soaring buzzards; and their flaunting flights along the airstreams. Daily, he saw the kestrel hovering, poised on the wind; the darting robin, inquisitive, watching the man's spade fling up the earth, eager for worms.

Tom could never understand how any man could ever be bored. Even when deep sorrow touched his life, the sight of kittens playing in the barn, or a small pig grunting as it hunted for milk, could bring a smile to his face and laughter to his eyes.

He had never known wealth; never had money to spare on luxuries; never had time to take a holiday. He was dedicated to his land and to his animals, to tending them from dawn till dusk; and he knew a satisfaction that no rich man would ever know. He brought life into the world.

He loved the sheep in his fields and the lambs jumping in excitement, so that often they ran, exultant, or played together and butted one another.

There was always something new to watch, as the small creatures discovered the world around them. This year one of the young males had found a loose piece of wood on a wire, dangling from the fence. It was part of a broken gate.

He spent hours butting it with his head, watching it swing, again, and again, and again. When any of his companions came to join the game, he butted at them jealously. The toy was his, exclusively, and he raced to guard it should one of the others, finding it free, try to play too.

The two men laughed at him. His need to keep his treasure to himself kept him so busy.

When the yard was cleared sufficiently to allow Tom to move easily to and fro, it was necessary to check the sheep. He whistled to Mel who came reluctantly, glancing behind her at the pups, running back to them and nosing them, then, at last, coming to his heel, obedient to his command. She worked for him without much will, longing to be free again, aware of the heaviness of the milk inside her, but she had a duty to perform.

Sam watched as she ran round the flock, and brought a ewe to her master, for him to pull a long thorny stick from the shaggy fleece. The stick was well tangled. Sam knelt, brought a pair of large scissors from the deep pocket of his duffle coat, and cut the wool away. The animal, freed from irritation, broke away, and trotted down the field bleating.

Number 19. The number was painted on her back. Tom watched as a lamb detached itself from a small group and raced to her. Maa, maa, maa. She answered it, her voice deep against its forlorn baby wail.

Number 19 on its back too. Tom nodded in satisfaction. He painted each ewe and lamb or lambs with identical numbers when the babies were born. It saved so much time if a lamb got lost.

"Back to your babies, lass," he said, and Mel, released, bolted across the field, wriggled under the stile and dashed back to the shed, where she settled herself to nurse, anxiously counting heads.

They were all there. She licked the last-born pup first. He yipped noisily, his voice drowning that of his smaller sister, who lay close beside him, trying to push him away so that she could feed. Mel shifted the little bitch to another teat, and nudged her close.

The whimperings ceased. There was only the sound of steady sucking.

"They'll be good pups," Tom said to Sam, watching her. "She's a grand bitch. She never lets me down, and she'll always work for me, even when she's aching to get to that litter of hers. A rare good mother."

A good pup. Sam licked his lips, aware of elation. His new pup would be nothing like Trip. This would be a pup to cherish; a pup with breeding; with his sire a past master at herding sheep, winning prizes at many trials, and a mother with a devotion to duty.

A pup to savour; a pup to dream about; his own pup. Sam longed for it but Tom would not let him take it till the training was started. He was to work with it here, under the eyes of an expert.

"I'll not let you ruin this one, the way Mervyn ruined Trip," Tom said.

THREE

SAM HAD learned the hard way that it was wise to listen to those who knew more than he. Tom had helped him save his little flock from disaster the year before. When the wind roared down the hill and the sea and the river met, the water backed up and flooded the fields.

"Get your sheep in," Tom had said. "That land will be under water by nightfall."

Tom had seen the signs in the moon, a full moon, decked with a glisten of cloud and a rainbow halo. He knew, from long experience, that there was trouble due, shown by the wild sunset, lurid light spilling across the heather. The piled-up threatening masses that darkened the horizon, shouting a warning that only a blind man or one new to the land could miss.

There was trouble spelled in the ominous thunder rumble from the far distance; and in the vivid lightning that flashed relentlessly across the sky.

The heavy clouds burst. Sam had never known such rain. Rain that lashed down in torrents all through the night. He woke to see his fields turned into lakes and ducks swimming where once the sheep had grazed, and thanked God that Tom had given him warning. He would never have believed it.

Tom had knowledge and Sam yearned for knowledge.

Dog knowledge. Sheep knowledge. The old man thought like an animal; knew the feelings that drove his bitch, and as soon as he was sure the sheep were safe he let her run back to her shed, back to her puppies, and settle with them.

Sam could not resist one last peep before he went home that night. Mel, aware now that he would not harm or touch, watched him, her bright eyes wary. The first glow of motherhood had dimmed, and she was willing to admit him into the shed. He bent to inspect his puppy; the last-born. The big puppy had black speckling round one eye, in an otherwise white face, except for a patched brown mark above both eyebrows which somehow gave him the expression of a comical clown.

An oddly marked pup.

A little pirate, he thought, and half decided to call the pup Pirate. But that was no name for a dog. The dog needed a good name; a name that would be remembered. This pup was going to make history.

Tom, coming to stand beside him, guessed his feeling. He smiled and asked "Well?"

"He's a super pup; a pup to dream about."

"Dreams only come true if you work at them," Tom said, but there was affection in his voice for this dark-haired hazel-eyed man with his powerful shoulders who could do the work that now defeated the older man. Age was a sad thing, coming to everyone, making life more difficult, making once easy tasks a penance. A man needed a son. Tom was glad that the young man had bought the farm next door. A bonus for his old age.

The day had become, briefly, warmer. A faint shine from a half-hidden sun triggered the lambs to leap over the hummocks in the field; to jump the molehills and to climb, one after another, on the little tump at the hedgeside, and stand there, before jumping down again. A mazy frolicking in which all but the youngest joined.

Then, just before sunset, there was a great bawling, with lambs bleating to lost mothers and mothers calling to errant lambs, until at last all were matched again, and the two men laughed at the busy sucking and the swinging, wagging tails, and the silence that succeeded the nightly panic.

There were red streaks across a lurid sky laced with black streamers.

"More wind tonight," Tom said.

"At least the trees are safe; there's nothing near enough the house to do you harm now." Sam looked up at the mountains. He was learning that here, where the weather changed fast from hour to hour, it was not wise to make forecasts.

"And plenty of wood for winter for both of us and no money needed to buy it. Always a silver side to the black clouds." Tom looked at the stack they had built that day. The woodpile meant money staying in the bank and not finding its way into the logman's pocket. The logman would have a thin time next winter.

"I'll bring food for Mel tomorrow; to feed my pup. I'd like to share," Sam said. Tom had refused money for the pup. A gift between friends, he said.

The old man nodded.

"He needs a name. And we must register him with the International Sheepdog Society."

Sam took one last look in the shed before he drove off in the battered old Land Rover he had bought at an auction a few weeks before. Hours spent cherishing it and replacing parts of the engine had given him a vehicle that would see service for several years, with care.

A puff of blue smoke from the exhaust lay in the yard for a moment and then drifted away on the wind. Mel watched it from the darkness. Sam was part of the farm and yet not part of the farm; a man who came often, yet was not given any of her affection.

There were no thoughts in her head; nor fear for tomorrow; only the deep passion for these, her pups, and the need that told her she must care for them with all the strength she had.

Tom fed her meat and biscuit, and then shut the door on her for the night. She lay in the darkness, secure, unafraid, and the last-born pup was the closest to her head, and perhaps the closest to her heart, for him she licked more than she did the others, having so nearly lost him.

Outside, among the misty stars, the moon crept over the horizon, a mere hint of a moon, a fragile crescent gleaming in the midnight sky. It filtered through the cobwebs on the tiny window and threw a finger of light across the small heads. Beneath its soft caress, Mel's flanks were piebald, the white fur on the pups conspicuous against the bitch's dark coat.

Mel herself was lean and black, her tail white-tipped. The father of the pups was a strongly marked black and white dog with a glossy dense coat, where hers was sleek and short.

An owl hooted, a fox barked higher up the valley, alerting Sam, who went outside to make sure his chickens were safe for the night. Mel listened too, aware that if the intruder came, she could not defend the hens and ducks, as Tom had made her door secure. A fox might take her pups and kill them. She needed to be safe from predators too.

The fox made his way up the mountain, to catch a rabbit on the hillside. His mate, a small dark brown vixen with a black-tipped tail, met him, and argued with him and won the argument, and took the trophy to her den, to share with the growing cubs that would plague the farms in the autumn. The fox went hunting again.

The biggest pup whimpered and wriggled and thrust his nose hard against his mother's side, drinking all she could give him, intent on growing even stronger. Mel lay with her nose on her paws, and slept.

Tom planned the pup's training, watching the moon creep over the sky, unable, as ever, to sleep well and soundly for long. Sam, younger, thought of his pup before he fell asleep, and dreamed he was working on a full-grown, handsome black and white dog in a sheepdog trial, with the sheep trotting, under full control, through each hazard, and the crowd roaring approval.

The pup, unaware of the great plans each man had for his future, nosed his mother, and slept, and dreamed, twitching, of milk.

FOUR

THE PUPS grew. As day succeeded day, Sam's first thought was to look at the litter. He had not watched a new-born litter grow before and was fascinated by each stage of the growth.

Within days the pups were noisy, crying lustily when Mel was with the sheep, shouting to her to return and feed them. They scrambled over one another, without any control of their legs; they gnawed on a brother's or sister's paw, hunting for milk. Only when they were fully fed did they lie quietly and sleep, a huddle of black and white bodies, with tiny paws that twitched in puppy dreams.

"Can't think what they dream of at that age," Tom

said, looking down at the nestlings. "Memories come with birth of rabbit running? Or just fear dreams of sucking and no more milk?" He teased at Mel gently with a wagging finger. "See you eat and drink and make good strong pups for me," he said, and Mel wagged her tail and grinned at him, her eyes laughing, knowing this man was teasing her.

Sam longed for the day he could take his pup out into the yard and play with it. He looked for it first, half afraid some disease might strike and rob him of his future. He had such plans for the pup.

The puppies lightened life. Both men stopped work to watch them; to laugh at them; to praise Mel, a first class mother who took her duties very seriously.

The days passed so quickly.

The biggest pup opened one eye first and stared at Sam when he came, looking even more like a pirate. The second eye opened a day later, and by then all the pups had one eye open.

By the third week they could see one another and see their mother and see the two huge men who towered above them. Two gentle giants, both amusing themselves by watching the games that now began.

The pups could crawl. They tumbled over one another, squealing and biting in play. Then they began to struggle away from the nest, to burrow in the straw, to lose themselves and cry forlornly so that their mother was endlessly busy, retrieving her adventurers.

Sam's pup, at five weeks old, found a short length of thick rope in a corner of the shed. He dragged it; he growled at it; he fought it, and his brother tried to take it from him. Instantly there was a fight; a puppy fight, snarls and growls and deep anger, and Mel came to her erring pair and shook each one soundly.

They nestled against her for comfort, dismayed by her wrath, which they had not met before. Sam and Tom, who had been watching, both chuckled to themselves as they worked, remembering the small furies, so tiny, so wild with rage.

"I once saw two young squirrels start a war over an acorn," Tom said, laughter in his eyes. "You never saw such a battle, or heard such a din. It's wonderful when they're small. They're so funny, and such little things make them mad with one another."

Sam laughed.

"I once didn't speak to my best friend for a week at nursery school because he wouldn't share his chocolate," he said. "He'd had half mine and promised me half his, and then ate all his. I thought it wasn't fair."

"It wasn't. But that's life, and people," Tom said. "Wonder what sort of dogs these imps will turn out to be?"

After Mel's scolding the rope end was shared, first one pup and then another toying with it. It was chewed. It was carried. It was tugged, one pup at one end and one at the other, growling, in play. The winner took his trophy and trotted off with it.

Mel sat, straddle-legged, watching her puppies, completely absorbed. Sam found them less and less easy to resist and spent many stolen minutes sitting on a bale of straw, whistling to the pups.

Tom, whenever he came into the shed with Mel's food, made a soft hissing noise, schwschwschwschw, between his teeth that brought all six small animals toddling over to him, eager now for his affection, learning that people were great fun.

By the time the pups were six weeks old all had been sold except the biggest pup. Sam wanted to take it home, but Tom felt it wiser to keep it on his farm for its early lessons.

"Can't run till you've learned to walk and nor can he; and young men aren't patient. Takes time to train a pup; and care; and thinking."

Time. Sam often felt there was no time. He was always impatient for tomorrow, for the dog to be trained, for the trophies they would win. Tom laughed at him, aware that time stretched. Once he had been twenty years old and eager for life. Now he was nudging seventy and had learned to savour each moment.

There was always time to breed another litter; time to rear a better pup; time to train a cleverer dog. Tom was always an optimist.

By his seventh week the pup was exploring the yard. He stared at everything he met, and then, having stared, he nosed it, smelling it, making sure that this scent was lodged in his memory for ever.

There were so many unknown things to smell. The path where the ducks walked. He did not at first associate it with the ducks. They ran from him, quacking noisily, never close enough to get to know.

The big pup was on his own and still without a name. He was endlessly inquisitive. He had to smell everything there was to smell; he knew where the chickens had run; smelled cat; shook his head in disgust at the smell of petrol in a puddle.

He nosed Sam when he came as if reading every inch of him. Nosed his hands, for the memory of food; nosed his legs, smelling Trip on the cloth, so that long before he met Trip he knew about the dog.

He tracked his mother endlessly, trying to follow her wherever she went and crying if she went out of his sight. Mel was tired of her duties and discouraged him when he tried to suck, snapping at him. A big boy now, her manner said.

He learned to feed from his own small bowl, though much went on the floor, which had then to be washed by his tongue. A lot of it clung mysteriously to his face, which his mother cleaned diligently, holding him still with her paw while he squirmed and complained noisily.

He learned, very fast, that if he dared put his nose near his mother's bowl, she snarled at him. Mel would never share her food, not even with her own pup.

He learned to chew on a bone, savouring the rich taste of meat that clung to it, growling softly at Sam when he came near, so that Sam knelt by the pup, and saying "no" to the growling, took the bone, avoiding angry little teeth, and then gave it back to the pup.

Within days, the pup was sharing his bone with Sam, offering it to the man, who was becoming very important to him. It was Sam now who brought the daytime food, and it was to Sam's soft whistle that he came fastest.

The little dog was nine weeks old when he found the file of baby ducks. He herded them, never allowing them to wander back to their mother. Neither Tom nor Sam saw this new game. The pup was totally absorbed. The ducklings had to be in a tight little knot; if one strayed he darted at it and brought it back again.

The game only ended when the mother duck, hunting her brood, flew at him with angry quacking and beating wings and sent him, in a panic, back to the shed, where he cowered in the straw, nose on paws, watching her take the little yellow bundles of fluff down to the pond.

But nothing could daunt the pup for long.

Sam returned to find him following a new trail across the yard, a trail left by one of the guinea fowl. The dog was so intent on the scent on the cobbles that he didn't even notice that the bird was only yards away from him, its smell being blown from him on a wind that was strengthening to bluster in the night and thrust the branches of the trees against the ground.

Sam whistled and the pup turned and ran to him, pawing against his legs, lifting his head in greeting, as he greeted his mother. Sam knelt and stroked the soft warm body.

The pup leaned against him, his expression blissful. He loved the touch of the men's hands. Then he stiffened. An immense black beetle was walking across the yard in front of him. He forgot Sam. He pointed his nose and ears at this extraordinary creature, then put out a paw and patted at it tentatively.

The beetle walked on and the pup followed, stalking it, so that Sam sat grinning, watching the little dog, so totally absorbed that he was unaware of anything else. The beetle vanished into a small crack in the stones, and the pup hunted for it, using his nose, in a desperate effort to trace this strange object that moved so enticingly, asking to be chased.

Sam whistled again. The pup ignored him, too interested in looking for other movements. Sam went to him, and gave him a little flick with his fingers, just behind the tail.

The pup woke to knowledge. The man wanted him, and he had disobeyed. Now he had to obey. Tom had put a tiny cat collar on the pup, and Sam fastened a piece of twine to it, and gave a gentle jerk and a soft whistle at the same time.

The pup had no choice; he had to come to the man.

Tom, watching, nodded approval. Even little pups had to learn to obey. No lesson could begin too soon, and once the pup had other thoughts in his head, then discipline had to start. No one could own a sheepdog that did as he wanted; Sam needed a better dog than Trip. He would have to watch that Trip didn't lead the new pup astray.

Each time the pup came to Sam he was fussed over, until he realised that this was a lovely game with rewards at the end of it. Sam had made a plait of fine rope, longer than the odd end that now lay forgotten in the shed. The pup pulled on it, small needle-like teeth gripping hard, small head shaking. A wonderful game that was very carefully played, so that the pup never came near the human hand and was never in danger of biting it.

He loved to nibble at fingers, but Tom's hands instantly encircled his jaws. A sharp no, and a little shake and he was beginning to realise people did not want puppy mouths against their skin. Except for the side of Sam's neck, which the pup was allowed to lick.

Once he nipped the man's hair and at once was given a little shake. No. Never. He was a bright pup and learned fast.

What to call him? Both men thought, over their coffee and their lunch-time sandwich, and both thought at night. Sam wanted an unusual name; a name that no other dog owned; a name that suited the pup.

The pup was nearly ten weeks old before they thought of a fitting name. He had learned to come to a whistle and to a cry of 'puppupupup, come', but as yet nothing seemed to suit him.

The name came one evening, just before Sam went home. The pup had vanished, and they hunted for him. He was not in the shed. They called Mel to find him for them, and she tracked busily round the yard, through the broken-down barn, and then to the chicken house. There was a small hole in the wood, and the pup was sitting by it, sniffing at it, and then watching the chickens, out of his reach. He moved as if he wanted to herd them, to round them up, and his eyes never left them.

"He's after anything he can spy," Tom said.

"Spy," said Sam. "We'll name him Spy."

He whistled and the pup came to him and wagged his small tail and pushed his nose against the petting hand, quite unaware that he was now a grown-up dog, with a name of his own that he would have to learn.

FIVE

SUMMER fled. The days were long and dry, and the two men spent much of their time carrying water to the troughs in the fields. There was little time for dog training. Haytime and harvests. Sheep that had to be sheared and dipped, and wormed, and examined for illness.

The work seemed to escalate. It was endless, the days always too short. Lambs broke down hedges, and Sam mended them. There were lambs to go to market.

Tom was weary, rheumatism plaguing him. His legs ached, and his breath came short and he often had to stop and rest. Sam, running two farms, became short-tempered and exhausted. He needed an experienced dog and not an untaught pup. Spy's education was neglected.

Spy did not mind. Life for him was all excitement. There were endless discoveries to make. Some of them were fascinating; some of them were surprising; some of them were terrifying. He was never quite sure just what life held in store for him.

Mel watched over him, teaching him, guarding him from harm, but she also played with him. When the two dogs were free in the yard there were endless games of tag, of romping and play-biting, and groaning at one another.

Mel, who, for the first time, had a daily companion for racing and fun, grew as skittish at times as her son and had to be reminded sharply that she was now a matron with duties to perform.

Sam had less and less time to spend with his pup. The weather appeared to have declared war on mankind. The scorching summer ended at last. It left the grass dry and fields denuded, so that money had to be spent on extra feed.

Winter came savagely and unexpectedly in early October. Hard frosts gripped the land.

The end of the hard spell brought no comfort. It was followed by days of rain. Christmas was a brief oasis, a pause for breath and then came January and a return of the bitter weather, with ice on the ground, and ice on the grass. The sheep were brought to the barns, lest the early lambs died. They needed bedding and they needed feeding and they needed cleaning. Job succeeded job, and Spy ran wild.

Ice had to be broken; on some mornings the troughs were solid within an hour of filling and the sheep unable to drink at all. The men carried buckets of warm water, which took hours they could ill spare. The ewes had to be brought into the barns to lamb.

Sam and Tom spent the whole of one day lining the biggest barn with bales of straw. They piled the bales four deep around the walls and then stacked them high, making a warm enclosure within which were the pens which separated one ewe from another and prevented those about to lamb from stealing babies that were not their own.

Spy, intruding unasked into the nursery, found that sheep were not as biddable as he had thought. He was met with lowered heads and angry stamping and large animals that shielded their new-born from this intrusive half-grown pup that had as yet no manners, and was apt to come too close, to eye too hard, and sometimes, if Tom did not see him in time, to nip at a woolly body.

Sheep fascinated the pup. He knew that he was meant to do something with them, and he watched Mel closely, sometimes copying her, but often, unable to contain his own energy, skidding madly round the herd, stampeding them, so that even Tom lost his temper and shut Spy in the shed.

"He needs training," he said daily, aware that time was speeding by and little pups became big dogs and this way Sam would have two dogs like Trip, not one.

If Mel were near she disciplined her pup, herding him away from the sheep, nipping him if he nipped a ewe.

Sam had his own farm and his own sheep; he worked from early in the morning until lunchtime there, and then came to check on Tom. Tom was tiring; nights spent with lambing ewes were ageing him. Sam worried, and spent half his nights with his neighbour's ewes and half with his own. He grew thin and edgy tempered, longing for the warmth of Spring, and a ceasing of the endless bitter winds.

One morning Sam drove to buy more straw; there was

not nearly enough. The ewes had to be kept warm or the lambs might freeze to death as soon as they were born. And there was extra feed to cart.

He called in for the pup. Time to introduce him to Land Rovers; to teach him to lie still while being driven; to show him the world beyond the farm.

The Land Rover was noisy. The soft top did not fit well and rattled and Spy did not like the movement; nor the noisy engine; nor being taken away from all that was familiar. He sat behind Sam and cried. He cried for company and for Mel; and for Tom; and because the cab smelled of strange creatures, not the familiar smell of his own sheep.

It was a disastrous journey and Sam wondered if this longed-for pup was going to be any good at all. It was hard to keep patient with the wailing from behind him, so that at one set of roadworks, where the red light persisted, he reached over and caught Spy by the scruff and sat him on the passenger seat, beside the closed window.

Spy stared at the world. He stared at houses and streets, and, to his surprise, saw other dogs on leads beside their owners and barked at them ferociously, warning them not to come near his car or his master.

It was the first time he had discovered a real bark and he enjoyed listening to himself, sure that this was a good thing, and that Sam would appreciate his vigilance.

Sam did not. Nor did he know how to stop the pup barking. When they reached the straw dealer's he tied Spy to the rear of the cab, so that he could sit and watch the world from ground level, and left him there.

The straw dealer owned a half-breed; part collie, part German Shepherd, a dog renowned for his fury with other dogs, and for his refusal to allow any dog on his patch. His name was Heinie. He smelled the wind.

A dog! On his territory! The door of his pen was not properly shut. The man who had put him away that morning was in a hurry. The dog leaped at the door, which opened; he raced down the yard and flew at Spy, who, fastened by his rope, was terrified, unable to run away.

His assailant was four times his size, and meant to teach this unwanted enemy a lesson he would never forget.

The men heard the snarls and the pup's agonised squealing. They pounded across the yard. The straw dealer grabbed his dog by the scruff of his neck, shouting angrily, and dragged him off.

Spy crouched, trembling, his mouth and ear bleeding profusely.

Sam lifted him gently, and comforted him.

"Sorry about that," the straw dealer said. "I didn't know Heinie was free; someone must have left his pen door open."

"Wouldn't like to meet him on a dark night," Sam said.

"Send me your vet bill. Hope the little feller isn't too badly hurt."

"More shocked than hurt," Sam said. "Won't do any permanent harm."

He didn't know how wrong he was until he walked into the vet's surgery with Spy on a length of rope at his side. Spy saw a dog his own size and before his master realised what had happened he had sprung, attacking him, anxious to prevent the dog hurting him first. He had learned, wrongly, that all strange dogs were dangerous.

Sam seized his pup, and carried him, raging, to the other side of the waiting room.

The vet had long experience of fighting dogs. He stitched the ear, which was badly torn at the base, and bathed the injuries on Spy's face, and gave him an injection.

Spy hadn't liked his first inoculations and he didn't like

this and growled.

"That's an upset you could do without," the vet said. "Have to watch him now. Every time a pup gets attacked, it teaches him other dogs are dangerous; and turns him into a fighter. People don't realise what harm their dogs can do to someone else's placid animal."

Sam did not yet realise how prophetic were those words, nor what that fight had cost him.

SIX

LIFE FOR Spy was all adventure. There were so many new things in the world; so many new smells to savour; so many discoveries to make.

Not all were happy.

He had always thought that sheep would, in the end, respond to his driving need to herd them. Would, if he stared them down and circled them, go where he wished, except for the penned ewes in the barn, now back in the fields.

Then he met a ewe – Bessie.

Bessie had lost her mother the night she was born. It was a bitter night and she, too, had nearly died, Tom brought her into the house, and into the kitchen and into the warm. And there Bessie proposed to stay, no matter how often she was evicted.

When Spy met her she was nine years old; and Tom regarded her as a cross to bear and also as a pet. Bessie regarded herself as a mixture of human and dog, having shared the shed in her early days with Tom's old sheepdog, Glenn.

She played with Glenn when she was young. To his dismay, Tom discovered as she grew, that she had no fear of dogs at all. She charged them, head down, baaing noisily, and no dog could ever herd her.

Mel never tried. Bessie was a law unto herself, parading the yard, venturing into the kitchen, stealing the bread, stamping angrily at the pup when he ventured too close.

Tom traded on her greed and when it was time for dipping or shearing, a trail of buttered scones led across the yard to her final destination, whether it was the shearing shed or the dipping trough.

Spy only tried to herd her once. He circled her and she charged, and kicked him in the ribs. Whimpering with pain, he ran to his bed in the straw, and did not venture anywhere near her again.

Yet, for all his fear of her, when Bessie did get into trouble, it was Spy whose need to save the stubborn old sheep led him into danger too.

One morning, putting his nose cautiously outside, he discovered a new kind of rain. Not the damp drizzling rain that seemed to have been falling almost daily for weeks, but rain that lashed in torrents out of a sky looming murkily overhead.

The distant mountains were hidden. The two men clumped morosely about their tasks, wearing streaming oilskins.

There was water everywhere. Water lay on the yard, one continuous puddle through which Spy splashed, mystified, unable to decide just where all the cobbles had gone.

The water deepened where the ducks swam and Spy could not see where the pools ended and the overflowing river began.

He was herding the ducklings, now half-grown and irritable with his chivvying so that one of them turned and faced him and he crouched and stared at it, willing it to move. It quacked at him and he barked back.

Bessie, who had been looking for grass, and was bewildered to find her grazing had vanished, turned to stare at the duckling.

It lost its nerve and ran and Bessie ran after it. She often behaved as if she were a sheepdog too. Spy, his own instincts triggered by all this activity, followed.

Bessie, venturing too far into duck territory, lost her footing, and the swirling water took her and swept her out into the current, her legs thrashing helplessly as the water soaked into her fleece.

Spy stared. One of his charges was being carried away. He jumped into the water, to retrieve the old ewe. He too was taken by the swollen stream and forced across the pond. He scrabbled desperately, finding in that moment how a puppy swam, with flailing legs that held him just above the surface.

Mel, always watchful, saw him paddling desperately, being pulled away from the bank, unable to make headway. She barked loudly, so that both men turned to look at her and then saw the floundering ewe and the small head trying desperately to reach her, and the struggles of the pup to perform his duty.

The river had grown in the night and was raging. It had torn down the fence, and spilled over the fields. Tom and Sam had spent long hours bringing the sheep to safety and now it looked as if Sam was going to lose his pup and the nine year-old sheep who was part of the farm and his life. He would miss both terribly if they drowned.

They should have shut both animals in. Spy was always inquisitive. Bessie, Sam thought, was half mad. She was always in trouble and cost them more time than they had to spare. She had fallen into a pit that Tom dug to fill with manure, the pile growing endlessly, with nowhere to put it.

She had climbed on to the pigsty in her younger days and fallen through the roof, much to the dismay of the old sow whose squeals of rage had fetched both men at a gallop.

Now she was floating among huge sticks, and a couple of drifting planks which were being tossed by the waves that were blown by a wind that had come from nowhere. It looked very much as if both sheep and pup would be lost. Sam ran, unable himself to see where the pond ended and the river began.

Mel, distraught, trying to reach her son, was also caught by the current and within seconds Tom saw his bitch swept away. Both dogs would be drowned. He ran, panting, and caught up with Sam who was knee deep, trying to stand.

"No good both of us getting into trouble," Sam said. "I'll take the old punt. Doubt if it's deep enough anywhere yet for me to be out of my depth. But if you fall. . . ."

Tom looked at him, agonised, hating the long years that added to his age and forced him to admit that he was no longer young. Inside he was a young man still, his brain ready to act, to will his legs to hurry; but his body disobeyed. He was tired, and he was cold; and there was work around the yard.

He watched the creeping water, looked at the hidden

hills and the sullen sky, and wiped his hand across his face in an effort to dry it.

That only made him wetter. Squelching, he tramped miserably back across the yard, aware that even in those minutes the water that had been ankle deep was now calf deep.

The farmhouse, and the barns around it, stood on a little knoll. As yet, his home was safe. Mel's shed, on a lower part of the ground, was awash. Straw floated out through the sagging door, which had been eased by the thrust of the water from its lower hinge. The dogs would have to come indoors tonight. That at least was safe from the floods. The old builders had known how the river could rage.

The punt was unwieldy, a lump of a boat that refused to do anything Sam wanted. He poled angrily, desperate to reach the animals. Mel, seeing him, turned and swam towards him, but terror had claimed Spy, who battled to keep alive and could neither see nor hear anything but the water that constantly flowed over his head.

He had long forgotten about Bessie, who had drifted to the far bank and climbed out, and was shaking her fleece.

Sam gripped Mel by the scruff and dragged her into the boat. She barked at him, and he turned clumsily towards the tiny-far off bump that was all he could see of Spy's head.

The pole stuck in the ground; the mud was deep and cloying and Sam, aware he had little time, cursed as he tried to drive against the stream.

Spy had given up. He was drifting, and then, quite suddenly, he was washed to the bank, to a shingly patch where the water lapped lazily and had, as yet, not covered the stones. He lay, panting for air.

Mel leaped out of the punt, and struggled ashore and lifted her puppy in her mouth. He was no longer a tiny animal, easy to carry, but strong and sturdy, more than half-grown. She stood, waiting, till the bow grounded, and then moved cautiously towards Sam who took Spy, and dropped him into the bottom of the boat.

Bessie was safe; she had lumbered off, discovering that here at least there was grass.

Mel jumped into the punt, and, with a savage thrust of the pole, Sam turned back towards the farm.

This time the current was with them. Tom watched in dismay as he saw that the water was still rising, and that, if it came any higher, his home might well be under more than the threat of flooding.

Then he realised, with relief, that the rain had eased, that the clouds were parting and, far away, there was a ghost of blue sky. The floods hereabouts went down as fast as they came and with the ceasing of the rain, the two men could relax again.

Sam tied the punt to a tree, and lifted Spy, wondering if the pup were still breathing. He was so still. His small body had been battered by tossing driftwood and he was exhausted.

There was only the faintest movement from his ribs, and he was very cold.

Mel stood by the steps to the kitchen, looking up at Tom. The house was forbidden territory, except by invitation, but there was no time to lose. The old man opened the door, saying gruffly, "Inside, girl," and followed her. He took a rough towel to rub her dry.

He banked the Aga, and threw another towel to Sam, who flung off his soaking coat, knelt on the rug, and began to work on the pup. It seemed hours before Spy sneezed and then whimpered softly.

"You little dope," Sam said, exasperated, as he realised that a light brown eye was watching him, and a soft warm tongue had just licked his hand. The dense coat was saturated. It seemed as if it never would be dry again.

Mel, her own coat as drenched, came to lie by the fire and to lick her puppy, one eye on Tom, ready to run if he told her to go.

"All right, girl. Get warm," he said, and she settled to her task, her tongue busy.

Tom looked down at them. Life without a sheepdog was unthinkable and if anything happened to Mel . . . he would have to keep a pup from her next litter. Spy could not yet work the sheep. The old man had no wish to borrow Trip, the unpredictable, likely to run off on a fox scent rather than herd the sheep.

"Time we started those lessons seriously," Tom said, leaning back thankfully in the creaking wicker chair. He had changed his clothes and lent Sam trousers and shirt and jersey which were too long and too tight for the younger man. Later, when the rain ceased altogether, they would get back to work. Meanwhile, Sam's wet gear steamed on the old wooden clothes horse, and his boots stood in a pool of water that Spy watched grow larger.

The pup was mystified. He could not understand where all the water had come from. He would never trust that pond again.

He slept, curled against his mother. It was a hard cruel world for a small dog. He sighed deeply and twitched his legs and whimpered in his sleep, and Sam wondered, as he drank scalding hot coffee and warmed himself, just what memories that episode would hold for both the dogs.

Later that day Spy ventured to the doorway and discovered, to his surprise, that there were patches of cobbles showing. He had no wish to battle with the water again. He kept to the far side of the yard, away from the pond, and it was weeks before Sam could persuade the pup to walk even as far as the gate, because the pond was beside it, and water, he knew, was treacherous and sucked small legs from under their owner and tossed small bodies hurtfully, carrying them far away from home.

Two days later, when the water had completely vanished, leaving behind it endless fascinating smells, Bessie wandered into the farmyard. She bawled for her treat of buttered bread.

Spy watched her. She looked at him as if recognising that he had tried to save her, and that night returned to the shed with the two dogs and settled with them in the straw. Spy discovered that her fleece was very warm indeed.

The rains eased. The floods subsided. The fields dried, and the sheep were put to graze again.

Spy explored, so long as he was sure he was on dry land. He skirted the puddles, not trusting them at all. Then came the first hint of summer. Lambing was ended. There was time again to spare for both men.

Spy's training was, at last, to begin.

SEVEN

TRAINING, Spy discovered, was not fun. He wanted to race round the sheep and nip their heels. That was fun. He wanted to see them charge down the field, in a tight angry mass. That was fun.

He wanted to sniff the ground for news of the creatures that had been there during the night; not only sheep, but birds and weasels and stoats and rabbits; hares and hedgehogs and a running fox that had dragged one of Tom's ducks across the ground. Tom hadn't missed it yet, but Spy knew that the intruder had taken one of their stock. That was not fun; it was an irritation, angering him.

Nothing must harm his charges and everything on the farm, he knew, was part of his responsibility.

As yet, Spy was too young and too inexperienced to know how to cope. He wanted to hunt the killer down. His instincts told him that here was an enemy, a threat to the farm, and the men with their insensitive noses were unaware of it. He tried to tell Sam, pawing urgently at his leg.

Fox, fox, fox, said his tense body and his urgent eyes. Mel knew what the pup was saying but she also knew that a good sheepdog guarded her flock in the field and did not run wild, hunting the foe. She snarled at Spy, who gave up trying to inform the men of his discovery. Tom did not realise the duck was missing until late that night, when he went to put the birds in their enclosures and lock them in safely.

The fox was young and bold but was also inexperienced. He had come hunting by daylight, seizing his chance.

Tom, looking in vain for his bird, cursed. It was a beautiful Muscovy, one of the farmyard characters, tame and absurd, coming to the kitchen as Bessie did for food, unafraid of the dogs, often marching into their shed and settling in the straw to preen its smart feathers.

Spy forgot the fox smell. He wanted to run in the sunshine and chase his tail. He wanted to play with Sam, not work with him, jumping up at the man, nipping in fun at his hand.

Tom watched them, but did not interfere. The old man was weary, feeling his age in aching bones and an intermittent shooting pain in his back, born of long years of humping heavy loads.

Though the day was warm there were storm-filled clouds on the hills threatening more heavy rain. Tom longed for his chair by the fireside. He was aware of an aching desire to rest, to lean back against the cushions and let the day drift past him.

Instead there was work to be done, and the sheep to herd out of the field. The grass was cropped short and needed time to grow again. Tom had hoped that Sam and Spy would move the sheep for him, but it was obvious it would have to be up to him and Mel. The bitch would never work for Sam, who, she knew, could not master her.

Tom leaned against the gate, watching, disappointment in every line of his face and in his considering eyes. He would give them another half hour before he took over.

Spy had youth in his heart and the scent of a bitch in his nostrils. The bitch at the farm three miles down the valley was shut away in the barn in season. News of her was born on a niggling wind that blew intermittently and teased the pup, now beginning to be a mature dog, but not yet knowing what these strange feelings were that needled him.

The scent on the air was enticing, calling him, rousing strange urges, and he savoured it, stopping work, his head up, his busy nose sniffing.

"Do as you're told, you little wretch," Sam said, anger and disappointment sharpening his voice. This was not how he had thought to train his dog. He had read every book he could find on sheepdog teaching, and had imagined the dog behaving as the authors said. Learning fast, obedient to his every word, so that the two of them were a team, the dog needing only the hint of a signal or a whispered command, or a soft whistle, to behave as the dogs on the television programme behaved. It looked so easy.

Dogs that gained so many points; dogs that kept the sheep moving gently; men that handled as if they and the dog were part of one entity and needed no teaching to perfect this routine.

Instead he seemed to have found himself an animal possessed of a demon, his mind full of anything but sheep. The anger in the man's voice unnerved Spy and he pawed at Sam's leg in anxious appeasement. He could not understand why the men ignored the messages on the ground and in the wind. Mel, with the wisdom of her years, had learned that many things that a dog knew passed the human kind by. There was so much she had tried, in her time, to tell Tom; and he had never understood her, even when she too, in her heady youth, had chased after an errant fox to try and recover the chick from his jaws.

Tom had not seen the fox trail; and never missed the chick, which had been hatched by the old hen who always nested in the hedgerow. Mel, when he found her crouched by the farmyard wall, aware of wrong-doing, afraid to come home, had been punished for her sin; and had learned then that her master could be very unfair. She had battled with the half-grown cub and it would never come near her territory again.

It was two days before Tom found three deep bites under her thick fur and by then they had begun to fester. The vet found four more. Tom thought she had tangled with another dog, and never guessed she had been trying to protect her charges.

That taught her, once and for all, that it was never wise to take her mind off sheep, no matter what was happening around her. She edged towards Spy, trying to warn him, but he was drowned in his own sensations and ignored her.

Sam knew nothing of the bitch down the valley; of the messages on the wind, or the heavy scent on the grass of blood from the dead duck, and the overpowering stench of the enemy that carried it.

Several times, when her son raced, out of control, Mel left her post and snapped at him.

Behave, you brash pup. Let the sheep go quietly, slowly; and never nip.

But Spy was young and over-keen and he forgot. Time and again, he forgot. It had happened so often before, in his earlier lessons, and the two men, lacking time and patience because of that, gave up trying with him and put him back in the shed and worked alone with Mel.

Sam, with far less experience than Tom, with so much hope for this newcomer, so much despair over his other dog, Trip, found it harder and harder not to lose his temper.

The sheep had to be moved. The pup had to obey. He knew what the whistles meant. But Sam did not realise he was moving his hands when he whistled, and that he rarely moved them in the same way twice. Spy, watching those busy fingers, now pointing, now sweeping towards the ground, now irritably drumming on any object that happened to be near, was bewildered.

Come, said those shifting hands. Go left, said the left hand but the voice said stand still. Go right, said the right hand, but the voice said come to me. The movements were so small that neither man was aware of them but the dog's quick eyes, looking for guidance, saw signals where no signal was given and became more and more unhappy. He could not understand why he was blamed. Those hands were far more important to him than the meaningless words. Sam had never realised that his dog did not yet understand human language, and Tom, preoccupied by his failing strength and by constant pain, had forgotten his own early training system.

Not even Tom realised that Sam's hands were giving the lie to the sounds that came from the young farmer's mouth. The dog was looking desperately for guidance and it was not there. He tried to work, aware that Sam was becoming angry with him and desperate to avert that anger.

Sam was never cruel and would never hurt his dog, but his body tensed, and the irritation that mastered him sharpened his voice, and the pup was fearful then. That too prevented him from learning.

Both men were puzzled by the pup's bad performance when with Sam. The younger man had not enough dog experience to realise he was expecting trained adult behaviour from an untrained young dog. Time alone would steady the pup who was filled with the heady feelings of youth.

Tom, used to his older dogs, four years away from having a pup himself, had also forgotten that young dogs did not come ready-made. He expected Sam's teaching to produce fast results, to produce a dog as steady as Mel, without remembering that Mel herself had been skittish in her youth, a merry pup that drove him at times to despair, sure she would never learn.

Tom knew he had to give the half-grown animal some leeway; had to gentle him, as Spy was a sensitive dog, alert to anger, and afraid of it even when it was only verbal. Spy was more sensitive than his mother, quicker to pick up anger in the men, and wary as a result of that. He needed praise to flower into maturity, but Sam was too inexperienced to use praise, and Tom too weary, wanting only to get the jobs done fast and get back to his chair and collapse into it, and ease his aching bones.

Mel was more of a stoic than her son and had learned that humans could be very unpredictable and often very inconsistent. Spy had not yet learned that and did not understand.

Sam tried again. It was important to move the sheep today and time was passing fast. The sun had shifted so far across the sky that the shadows of the trees lay across the field instead of along it.

Spy, aware of irritation, tried very hard. Slowly, slowly, slowly. One false move, one fast rush, and the flock would be scattered all over the field again. He crept, belly flat against the ground, his eyes on the sheep in front of him, but a gale was growing, the trees already shivering at its touch. Its unseen breath blew his fur and he became wind-crazy, running in circles, maddened by this invisible giant that thrust at him out of nowhere.

He hated wind. It was inexplicable; unseen, noisy, with an overpowering medley of scents of all kinds that filled his nostrils and made it impossible for him to distinguish one smell from another.

It drove the scent along the ground so that it was far from its source, bewildering him when he hunted a track, and could find nothing at the end of it. There should have been a sheep, or a lamb, but the creature making the scent was far away from him.

The heavy mass of dark cloud foretold rain. Rain in torrents that would make work a penance and Sam wanted the sheep moved fast. Impatience made him careless, and he longed to take the pup and shake some sense into him. He did not want to give the task to Tom and Mel.

He wanted to do it himself, to do it well and have Spy work well for him.

Spy was too young. It was impossible to be slow, to be steady, to be patient. The sheep knew the dog was inexperienced and they tormented him. They could not outface Mel, who had learned how to cope with their resistance to her driving, but this newcomer was easily put off by a stamped hoof, or a head down charge.

Also the lambs were skittish, with the breeze under their tails and a merriment still in them not yet deadened by age. They leaped and jumped over the hummocks, never still, and Spy, tormented by the smell of the bitch, infuriated by the unmannerly behaviour of his flock, puzzled by Sam's busy hands, became wilder and wilder.

Everything inside him was at war. The bitch scent confused him. Then a ewe moved, slowly, as the pup briefly obeyed Sam, having understood at least one command. Lie down. He dropped. The sheep turned and looked at him, and her gaze faltered. He crept forward, eyeing her, and she began to move in the direction Sam desired.

In that moment Spy began to understand what herding meant but his keenness overrode his sense. Then the wind, strengthening fast, betrayed him. The wild branches bent and moaned and the steady roar bemused him. His desire to please Sam was counteracted by the now overwhelming scent from the other farm as it was blown continuously towards him.

The wind worried the sheep. They turned from it, ran from it, ignoring the dog, making for the shelter of the distant hedge which would protect them from those seeking fingers that drove into their fleeces, and chilled them. They were further than ever from the gate.

Spy tried, aware of Sam's mounting anger, anxious to divert it, knowing something was required of him, but the task was too hard for him. It was so difficult to lie still, when the sheep were running. When they galloped, then so did he, speeding round them, often herding them in the wrong direction.

Tom, waiting to open the gate, to let the flock through into the second field, waited in vain. Spy never had them bunched and moving as they should move.

Now one, and now another, broke away.

A group of lambs tumbled and skipped towards the fox gap, which neither man had seen. Mel saw it, and left her post by Tom's side. Her master wanted her to lie still to see if the pup could master the sheep and drive them as they should be driven. She knew that a fox had run across the field while the men breakfasted, and she flew towards the break in the hawthorn, knowing the sheep would be through.

Tom whistled her back, annoyed with her for disobeying him, unaware that she was doing a job for him, was telling him of the breach in the hedge. She hesitated, her affection for her master telling her to obey, her need to prevent the flock escaping telling her to disobey. In that second a lamb was through and then a second and then a third.

Within moments the gap was breached. The hedge around it was broken. The whole flock streamed merrily into the cattle field, where young heifers bolted, and triggered Spy who raced at their heels, snapping.

Tom pulled himself off the gate, which he felt was all that prevented him from dropping to the ground. He walked towards the hedge. There were feathers, now trampled into the ground, in the gap, which told their own tale. One of his ducks? He didn't as yet know.

More work and a hedge to mend. He whistled to Mel, but until Spy was caught and removed there was no hope of quieting the mêlée. The pup was racing at the sheep and at the cattle, snapping at flying hooves, turning a herding into a riot.

Sheep bleated in noisy chorus, drowning the sounds of the gale. Lightning flashed, splitting the sky, and all the beasts ran. Spy fled in terror, but could not find a place in which to hide. The roaring rumble of thunder frightened him even more. The heifers, equally alarmed, unused to dogs, were milling.

Spy, aggravated by the blazing light that flashed intermittently and unexpectedly, ran from the stampeding hooves and total chaos of animals fleeing in all directions. He bolted towards the far gate, leaping it in one flying movement, and jumped through the Land Rover window, where he crouched under the bench at the back. Here he was in the dark. He trembled with fright every time the skies split open, the light blinding him. He was even more afraid of the thunder rumble that crashed and echoed on the rain-soaked hills.

Tom, soaked to the skin, drove Mel relentlessly into the melée. Worst of his worries was that this was his neighbour's field and Jim Latten would have a good deal to say if he came and caught them; especially about the broken hedge. That boundary was a source of irritation to both men. Lambs were adept at finding gaps that men believed too small for them. They were always escaping.

Usually the men were warned by the frantic maaing of the stray outside the field, unable to find a way in, and the desperate bleating, deep and urgent, of the mother, as she raced up and down the hedge bottom, trying to make contact with her erring offspring. Tom had intended, for years, to fence it as well as layer the hedge, but there was little enough money and never enough time.

Time.

They had to get the sheep out of the field and the hedge blocked as soon as possible. Sooner. Jim was away delivering cattle food but would be back in the early afternoon.

They must get the sheep out.

They needed two dogs. Sam ran to the Land Rover, dragged the pup out, and fastened a thin cord to him. Spy had to work. They couldn't manage without him.

Spy, terrified by the strange behaviour of the world, by the flashing zigzags of light that cut the clouds, by the deafening clatter that followed it, had only one desire and that was to get back to the relative safety of the Land Rover.

Sam dragged at him. The thin line which attached Spy to his master broke, and as the dog snatched himself away from restraint, the cord cut the palm of Sam's hand, so that pain added to his anger. He bellowed at the dog.

"You hateful little beast. Come here."

His voice sounded above the bawling of the beasts; echoed from the mountains and stopped even Mel in her tracks. Spy, appalled at such rage coming from a human mouth, did not dare to disobey. He was as terrified of the anger which Sam could barely hold in check as he was of the storm.

He crept towards his master, ears flat, body abject, and lay at his feet, his bright eyes desperate with pleading.

"He's young," Tom said.

Sam looked down at his pup. Spy was soaked, his fur draggled and muddy, rain streaming from him. The sky split open again and the thunder blast that followed on its heels deafened both men. The pup was shaking.

"He's never heard that before," Tom said. "Mel knows about storms."

Mel, as wet as her pup, was unhappy but knew there was work to do. She had stopped listening to Tom's commands. His whistles were drowned by the wind and the thunder. She knew exactly what was needed and was working in her own way to sort the sheep from the cattle.

Sam swallowed his wrath. He knew the dog's behaviour was as much his fault as Spy's. He hadn't started to train him early enough; he hadn't insisted but had given up when his patience died; time had been against him, but he should have made time.

He lifted the dog. Better to carry him out of the field than risk him getting loose again and adding to their troubles. He did not realise that the dog had only one desire now and that was to hide from the world that seemed to him to have gone crazy.

Tom, cursing the weather, moved quietly and very deliberately, watching every move of dog and sheep. Mel soon had the flock under control, isolating them from the cattle, herding them back through the gap, across the grass and towards the gate where she held them bunched while Tom opened it and let them stream through.

Sam watched, envious. He wished he had that skill and Tom's placid nature, but he, like his dog, was young, and had to conquer his own impetuousness.

"Oh Spy, Spy," he said, later that evening, when they both were dry. Spy had been coming back with him for nearly two weeks now. Sam had brought the pup indoors. He was soaked and shivering and afraid of the distant booms in the air that still startled the night. Sam was ashamed of his own lack of competence, ashamed of his unruly sheepdog, and envious of the old man's ease with Mel. "What am I going to do with you?"

Spy, warm and dry, no longer bothered by the news of the bitch down the valley as the wind had changed direction, leaned blissfully against his master's leg and tentatively licked his hand. He could sense the disappointment, and knew it was directed against him but he could not understand it.

Later that night, when the storm sounds had ended, Sam put the dog in his shed, the door shut firmly on him. Just before morning the wind changed its direction yet again. The pup sat beneath the window, scenting the air that blew through the cracks, telling him news that the men would never understand. There was a bitch waiting for him far down the valley, if only he could escape. He was as much in love as any teenager suffering unrequited pangs, coveting a girl who would never even look at him.

Escape was impossible.

Sam, waking from his sleep, heard the dog's wolf howls as he cried for a bitch as unobtainable to him as was the moon. A few minutes later, Trip, sleeping behind the barn, caught the scent and joined in. Sam cursed both his dogs for ruining the silence of the night.

"The Tremayne bitch," Tom said next day when Sam told him. He remembered broken nights of his own. Remembered also the postman had said the bitch was in season and the Tremaynes were hoping to have a litter of pups from her and one of the more famous of the present sheepdog champions.

It was a long time since the old man had worked a dog. He preferred bitches. They didn't go off hunting when the wind brought them news of a possible mate. He hadn't heard that noise since Rip died, some twenty years before. The old dog had been a demon, living up to his name. He was the only dog Tom had ever had that made the night hideous with his moaning whenever there was a bitch nearby. He had even howled for a young bitch down the valley the night before he died; too old almost to walk, but not too old to respond to that. He had howled forlornly, the howls growing weaker, and when Tom had come at last to look at him the dog had wagged his tail feebly and closed his eyes for the last time.

It had been a good peaceful end and Tom hoped he had died happily, dreaming of his past conquests.

Tom's other dogs hadn't bothered; some dogs shouted and some did not and Spy was obviously a dog that would not endure his misery alone. Others had to hear of it.

Spy was left in the Land Rover; the gap in the hedge had to be mended, and there was work to be done and the pup was in the way. The intermittent wolf howl went on all day, irritating both men and unsettling Mel.

Sam, irritated by the noise, was not sure he even wanted the pup now. His dreams were shattered and it looked as if he would be the laughing stock of the neighbourhood with two untrained animals instead of just one.

The dog was quite unteachable.

EIGHT

"TIME WE took a few hours off," Tom said, one bright morning when the sun promised a fine day. Little clouds danced in the sky, but there was no sign of rain. The hills were a blue haze, softened and distant, no longer the threatening winter giants that killed so mercilessly when the unwary ventured on their treacherous slopes.

"Sheepdog trials over on the Tremayne Farm. Do you good to see how a dog should be handled. We'd best leave the dogs behind. Mel always wants to join in. Knows she can do it better," Tom said, and chuckled. "Spy's still not safe with other dogs. Our fault, that."

They raced through the necessary work. Tom went

indoors and reappeared looking as if he were bound for church. Dark suit, and neat tie, and a new cap that was slightly too small for him. He tipped it back on his head, and squinted at the sky.

"Going to hold." He looked with approval at Sam who had driven home and returned in new corduroys and a pigskin jacket that had cost more than he ought to have spent, but that he had coveted.

"Smart as paint, both of us," Tom said, as he padlocked the door of the shed. A good dog was a bonus to a thief and worth several hundred pounds if trained.

The trials field sloped to the horizon. The judge and stewards stood, important, the judge holding his clipboard. He was a stranger to Sam, a farmer from the other side of the hills, brought in to judge men he did not know. Fairer that way.

Dogs stalked beside their masters. Men with crooks grouped round the tea van, or bought hotdogs, and the talk was of sheep and of dogs. Good dogs, bad dogs. Dogs that did their job and dogs that shirked it.

Sam, standing by the stone wall, knee deep in long grass, watched a lean black collie race out to herd his sheep, and fail to find them. The dog cast, back and to, back and to, and then, tail down, left the slope and came to his master.

"Wind's wrong," Tom said. "Catch a lot of dogs, that will. And it's gusting." He looked at the streamers in the sky. "A lot of wind. It'll grow during the day. Drives all the dogs crazy."

Sam thought of Spy, racing in heady circles, his fur almost on end, blown by something he could never understand.

There was a girl moving out now, a red-headed girl, walking proudly, full of confidence.

"Charlie, Jacko's granddaughter," Tom said. "Watch her. She's good with her dogs. Bred that little one herself. Only a titch of a dog, but my word, she's fast."

The little black and white collie sped uphill, casting. She crossed the wind, caught the scent of her sheep and began to drive them. Charlie whistled and whistled again; again, and again. The dog crouched, then crept on, never hurrying, moving smoothly, almost gliding.

She finished to a roar of applause.

A second woman went out.

Sam recognised Charlie's mother, Max. He barely knew them. He was shy and there was little time, and what free time he had he liked to spend playing darts and listening to the farming talk in the bar at night.

Max was a better and more experienced handler than her daughter. Handling quietly, the dog losing so few points that the applause this time was even louder.

Sam, watching, was envious. If only he could work Spy like that. Maybe one day.

Tom had regained his vigour, arguing about the dogs, picking out his favourite. No time for a wall-eyed dog, or a light-eyed dog, he said. The other men in the group, laughing at him, accused him of prejudice, of an old man's habit of believing old wives' tales.

"Best dog I ever had was a wall-eye," one of the Tremayne men said.

"I don't like a dog that won't look you in the eye," another said.

"Doesn't do to stare at a strange dog. Might attack," Tom said. "Your own dog now, that's different, but even so I've known a couple that would jump you if you looked at them. Old Matt, he had a temper, that dog. Never bred from him. Couldn't trust him."

The talk washed over and round Sam. Half the time

he wasn't even sure he followed it. The men became technical, using words he had never heard before.

The day ended with Max tying first with a young farmer from down the valley, and Charlie coming second. The women passed Sam, laughing, their dogs leaping round them, knowing they had done well.

He wished he could approach them, and ask them how they trained their dogs so well, but shyness held him back, and he only nodded to them as they went by.

That evening, walking home after his darts game, he vowed that he would train his dog until he could beat both the women, and the shepherd who had tied with Max. When Sam slept he dreamed of dogs, and of men who whistled continuously to them, the soft noise echoed in the wind that savaged the hills and caused Spy to creep closer to Mel, seeking comfort, as he lay in the straw.

He hated wind, whether he was indoors or out. It was worse indoors, as it sang round the shed, making eerie noises that caused Spy to think there were great beasts out there, waiting to jump him.

Sam studied his books. He tried, night after night, to train his pup. He remained unaware that his hands belied his voice; and that sometimes his body did also. Spy moved fast and Sam could not outthink him; he needed to say "no" but it invariably came out too late, after the misdeed had been committed.

Spy was bewildered because Sam said "no" when he was doing right; and so what he thought was right was wrong. He was becoming more and more confused and more and more anxious. Neither attitude helped him learn. Sam's own disappointment did not help either. He was sure he was working with the dog, was doing well himself and the dog was at fault. No book could tell him what was the matter with his training.

He needed an expert to teach him how to train his dog, but did not know that and in any case did not know where to find one. He was an obstinate man who hated to give up on anything; who hated to be proved wrong or to admit defeat or a fault in himself. He was aware that Tom was a better trainer, but put that down to Mel being an easier dog than her son.

Shame at his failure prevented him from asking at the other farms in the valley. He was an incomer, a city man turned farmer, and he was sure they were all waiting to see him fail and go back to his former life with his tail between his legs.

He did not intend to give them that satisfaction. He worked on, alone, making more mistakes, making matters far worse for both himself and the dog, and neglecting Trip who became even more unruly, lacking any guidance at all.

There was all his own farm work to do as well as Tom's as the old man was becoming feebler and often slept late and was hard to rouse. He sometimes stared at Sam with a bemused expression as if he did not know him. Sam had to lock up the birds before he left or they were still out in the morning and the fox had been busy. He ceased to lock Mel in the shed. She soon came into the house with her master, and Tom did not remember that he had ever shut her away. Her head against his ankles was comforting; and she slept now by his bed each night.

Again and again Sam read his books. Training, as laid down in them, looked so easy. The writers had never had a dog like Spy; a dog that had a mind of his own and a will of his own and a mental block against learning. They wrote as if every dog were the same and could be programmed the same way. They did not mention the problems in training; the things that went wrong, and their cures for mistakes were missing.

They gave time limits. Three weeks and the dog would understand; five weeks and the dog would be well taught; within months the dog would be working with the sheep, obedient to the whistle, never failing.

The books were written by experts; by men who had won in trials or trained sheepdogs for years. Sam did not realise that many of them would have discarded Spy; would never have dreamed of keeping him or of trying to teach him. They would have sold him, perhaps as a pet, and bought a more submissive animal. And many of them started with part-trained dogs that other men had guided first and assessed.

They hadn't time to master a difficult dog; they sought for dogs that had come from good breeding, had been carefully picked out of the litter, had shown, from the start, that they would be excellent with the sheep. And if they failed, then goodbye.

Sam was unaware of all this, and Tom, though he knew it, had forgotten it. He had bred his own dogs for years and taken the easiest; and sold the rest. He had thought Spy would be an easy dog; and he had been proved wrong. There was always one that proved you wrong. Like Sam, it didn't occur to him to get rid of the pup now that they had started with it.

Sam did have the sense to keep Spy away from Trip. The old rogue would lead the pup astray, and Trip was a rogue. He had been cheap, and that should have alerted Sam, but as yet he was not used to country ways, or country wiles.

There must be some secret, but Sam didn't know where to find it. He used the books as a blueprint, lacking the experienced dogman's instincts.

"Come," he'd call, tense and angry because Spy was uneasy about approaching him. He never realised that the dog was becoming afraid of him, or that he should have used far more praise on this particular animal and welcomed him with pleasure every time he obeyed the command to approach.

Spy was an odd mixture; his hearing was unusually sharp, so that he heard sounds long before even Mel was aware of them. He was sensitive to voices, needing a gentle soft tone all the time, shying away from Sam's briskness and curt hard commands.

Trip needed a much harsher voice than Sam ever used; he was a bold dog, his own dog, a boss dog, unwilling to give way to humans. He knew every movement that Sam made, knew just how far he could go before wrath descended; knew when Sam was overtired and unwilling to exert authority.

He and Spy had little to do but study their owner, but where Sam's inconsistency gave Trip a lever he could use, it merely worried Spy, who needed to be bossed. Trip didn't. There was a wildness in him that would never be mastered. Though, had he belonged to a much more determined man who had earned his respect, Trip would have been a very rare dog indeed and a very good one. Sam was not yet experienced enough to recognise Trip's dominance, or to understand that Spy was merely anxious and confused.

Tom was obsessed by his own fears, aware that his body was betraying him. The weariness which, earlier in the year, came over him late in the evening, now overwhelmed him at four in the afternoon so that every move after that was a major penance.

The old man would have to sell the farm; would have to give up his life's work. Would have to live elsewhere, among strangers, and end his days without the beasts to gladden him. He loved his beasts and spent time now watching the lambs, growing into staider animals, as they frisked in the fields; watching the ducks on the pond; watching Mel when she was free from her work, nosing the ground, asking it to tell her its secrets, and coming to him satisfied, knowing things he could never ever know.

He did not tell Sam. If he kept his fears to himself, told no one, then perhaps they would go away. Proven unjustified. It was a temporary exhaustion, come at the end of the winter lambing and the problems they had trying to train Spy, and the way the day's work had been extended, time and again, through the pup's unruliness.

"He'll never make a trials dog," Sam said one morning. Spy no longer howled all night. He had lost his happy easy manner, lost his busy wagging tail, that now often drooped at half mast. He had developed a wariness that Sam could not understand, a habit of working, though only when he chose and if the mood took him, with one anxious eye on his master, as if he found him unpredictable.

Tom, a few years before, might have recognised what was happening. Now he was too engrossed in keeping himself moving, in spite of a constant tormenting ache in his back. It took all his willpower to get through the work and not let Sam guess at his increasing infirmity.

It was a forlorn attempt as Sam was well aware of the fact, but reluctant to discuss it, not knowing how to tell the old man that his days on the farm were numbered. It was no longer possible to run the two farms.

There was far too much to do, and no money for any paid help. Both men hoped against hope the circumstances would change, that some miracle would happen. That they would not need to make any decision. Sam struggled on, growing more and more weary, his temper shorter, his dog becoming afraid of him, of the anger in the man's voice, which Sam could not always hide.

The weather had turned against them, too, the summer betraying its name. It was cold and often wet and they squelched through the muddy fields and handled the dripping sheep and the pond overflowed into the yard and made life even more difficult. The foxes came by night and by day and took the birds when they chose, as if they knew the men were stretched beyond endurance and the sly animals were mocking them.

Sam grew to hate the foxes. Tom, when he was well enough to care, hated them too and set traps, but the cunning beasts were too wily and took another route, recognising the hated smell of man on the wood.

One morning they shut Mel in, and took the pup by himself, hopefully, as Tom knew Sam had been working with him. They went to the far field, to bring the sheep to the yard for dipping. One of the men from the local Fair Trading Office was due to supervise. The sheep needed to be down in time.

Twice Spy stampeded them, so that they bolted to the wrong end of the field, defying the dog. Tom had to fetch Mel and have her herd them back again. Spy refused to come when he was called. Sam's anger had mastered him again and the dog did not want to come too near. He knew he would be lifted roughly and thrust into the Land Rover and left there for the rest of the day. The field held much more interest.

Spy did know the meanings of the words. Come by. To me, and the whistles. He just could not bring himself to heed them. And sometimes there were much more interesting smells on the ground than those of sheep. Rabbits. Hares. The grass where the partridges had spent an hour feeding. They all needed investigation.

Tom shouted at Spy as the pup sped in to harry a ewe that refused to join her sisters. She bucked and stamped at the dog and he leaped and snapped at her ear.

"He's a disgrace," Tom said, bitter at having kept the wrong pup. Spy's brother was settling well on a farm further down the valley and high reports of his skill came to them. Neither man remembered that the other pup was in the hands of a skilled trials man and neither knew that the pup too was a different nature from Spy, much more biddable, much easier to manage, much more willing to learn, and far less easily distracted as sheep to him were the be-all and end-all of his day.

He had been taken young and taught young. Spy had learned there were other things in life much more interesting than sheep. He had run free too much and too long.

Tom had forgotten how important were those first few months and Sam had never known.

"How did it happen?" Sam asked. "What have I done wrong?"

"We maybe left him too long," Tom said. The sun had come out and brightened the day, and his back was less painful. He had a rare moment of insight. "Should have started training weeks before, to keep him calm; he's run wild, learned bad ways, been left on his own too much. But he's also a wild pup; takes after some long-ago ancestor. You never can tell with breeding."

Sam bought yet another book on sheepdog training and pored over it. Perhaps this man would have an answer. He was a well-known competitor in the trials world, having had successes with many dogs.

Sam read late at night; there was no other time. He read the words over and over with painful intensity, longing to make sense of them, longing to learn from them. But there was only a tale of success and more success, of dogs that never made mistakes, that grew into famous dogs, wonderful animals with instincts put there as all sheepdogs' instincts were. Instincts that seemed to have passed his dog by.

As Tom aged, and the work became more and more demanding, Sam's feelings defeated him. Spy was his dog and he would never be cruel to him; he couldn't sell him to anyone else. For one thing, no one else would take him. Sam knew he was now the laughing stock of the valley.

With Spy and Trip together he owned the two worst dogs in the country. He had no idea how to get himself out of the trap he had made for himself.

NINE

CHARLOTTE Leigh was a big girl; a redhead with a flashing smile, a quick flaring temper and a ready wit. Her relatives said she had been born in a kennel and that was almost true as her mother, Max, had been sitting with a whelping bitch until it was obviously time for her to go off to the hospital.

Max had worried more about the bitch, left in inexpert hands, than she had about herself. She came home when Charlotte was only two days old to supervise the rearing of the litter.

Everyone called Charlotte Charlie. Her mother being known as Max, added to the confusion. Strangers expecting to find two men found two women, and both feminine women at that, in spite of their names.

Max, who had been christened Maxina, had long forgotten her real name and so had Charlie. They lived among dogs, and talked of little but dogs. Both trained sheepdogs. Max was a formidable opponent, respected, and perhaps a little resented, by the men. Charlie was determined to beat her mother, and couldn't wait for the day.

It was a friendly rivalry.

"I taught her all she knows," Max said with satisfaction if told her daughter had a better chance than she at the next trials. Everyone knew their two best dogs. Charlie had named hers Havoc, intending to create havoc among the competitors and win all the prizes. Max's bitch was named Dish, a name that puzzled many people and reduced mother and daughter to laughter when they were asked about it.

Neither ever explained.

Dish, when only able to crawl, had fallen out of the whelping box and into the huge dish in which was her mother's dinner. Her mother, a greedy animal, had eaten the food before washing her baby. Max had found the pup in the middle of the dish, complaining bitterly, while the bitch ate everything around her.

Once that was gone, she lifted the squalling mite, took her into the box and cleaned her up thoroughly.

The puppy that fell in the dish became Dish and remained that way, even when she was winning the local trials and Max was dreaming of more heady delights and bigger victories.

The valley accepted the two women, though they often laughed at them, and the more sober matrons were sometimes shocked by them. Sensible women didn't have names like Max and Charlie nor did they campaign dogs christened Havoc and Dish.

Nor did they roar with laughter when found in odd situations such as on the day that Max had fallen into a pan of clay which she had been using to cure her pony of laminitis. The vicar had called to ask for help with the flowers the following Sunday. Max was as likely to win first prize at the local flower shows as she was to win with her dogs, and her garden was famous. The bishop was visiting on Sunday and the vicar wanted to fill the church with bounty. Max, though a rare churchgoer, was always generous.

The vicar, a small solemn man with a bald head causing him to be christened Egg by the children, found himself confronting a grinning grey shape, leaning, helpless with laughter, across an equally slimy pony. Charlie sat on the edge of the horse trough filled with marigolds, equally helpless with laughter, tears streaming down her face, unable to speak.

"Mad as hatters, both of them," the vicar had said later at tea to his wife. "But you can't help liking them."

His wife, much less charitable than he, disapproved of them both. She poured another cup of tea and said nothing.

Nice women didn't talk about mating dogs as if it were a normal subject for conversation. Max and Charlie always seemed to be mating one bitch or another to some famous dog and raving over the resulting litter. Their pups were sought after, and Max's trained dogs fetched high prices.

Charlie's father had been an equally odd character, earning himself many raised eyebrows as he could never resist pulling staid and solemn legs or puncturing the pompous.

He had been in the Royal Navy and was rarely home. He descended on them at intervals, filling the house with bustle and laughter and excitement. He had a formidable energy which his daughter had inherited. He was always loaded with presents for both of them, treating them as precious parts of his life, teasing his small daughter, whom he adored.

He told her fantastic stories, inventing strange tales about the foreign people and places he visited that she found entirely believable.

Once he told her that there was a race of men in Africa who trained pygmy camels to herd cattle, just as a sheepdog did in Britain.

Charlie, fascinated and only six years old, had written this in an essay and been challenged by her teacher as a liar when she had maintained it was the truth. After that she had refused to believe any story her father told her, never sure if her leg were being pulled or not.

He had died when Charlie was ten years old. His ship caught fire. He won a medal for gallantry, saving his men, carrying the injured, not leaving until it was too late.

He had never been home for long; and though his wife and daughter grieved for him, they were used to being without him and life went on.

Charlie never forgot his stories, but when she was older she checked his statements carefully. She understood his trick of mind and had her own ways of teasing but he had, accidentally, taught her to form a habit of verifying everything she was told. She did not intend to be caught again by repeating one of his fictions as fact.

Gossip, she discovered, was often based on guesswork. Or on spite. Or pure invention out of boredom, and though there was often a grain of truth, everyone built on fact and made up a falsehood.

Sam hated women, the gossips said. Been jilted, no doubt, or maybe married and his wife had left him. He had come to live in the shadow of the mountains to mend a broken heart.

Neither Charlie nor Max had much patience with gossips.

Charlie, always curious about her neighbours, had watched Sam with his dog, unknown to him, and was itching to show him what he was doing wrong. "Nothing much wrong with the dog," she said briskly to her mother, "but, dear heaven, you never saw anything like the man. He hasn't a clue."

"Don't interfere," said Max, "He won't like it. And you are younger than him by at least five years." Her daughter stared at her in astonishment. What had her age to do with anything?

Charlie waited. The moment would arise, and besides, Tom needed more help than just Sam. She watched the old man grow feeble, and more stooped. He walked wearily when he came to the village and moved as if his body hurt all over. She had seen old dogs go the same way; everything giving out. Old age wasn't kind to man or beast.

Charlie was possessed of a deep sympathy and a need to mother any creature that came under her care. And a few that didn't.

She had every intention of interfering, but not in such a way that Sam would cast her out of his life in fury and have nothing at all to do with her. She lived a few hundred yards down the road from his farm, and their land adjoined.

Sam, always shy with women, had little to do with Max or her daughter. He was brusquely polite, colouring violently if either of them spoke to him. Women terrified him with their strange ways, their odd sense of humour, their unpredictability. His mother had been more unpredictable than most; a butterfly woman, flitting from subject to subject and thought to thought, so that Sam never quite caught up with her.

Spy made a meeting possible. Havoc was in season, and the dog escaped from his shed. Sam, in a hurry, and overtired, had not shut the door properly. Spy raced out, and followed his nose and the scent on the wind, and arrived with a couple of other eager dogs at the kennel door.

Spy had been taught young that other dogs were dangerous and might hurt him. The lesson the straw yard dog had taught him had sunk as deep as the bites he had suffered. He was not going to suffer again.

He attacked the biggest dog, a lean rangy animal that fathered many village pups and had no intention of letting this newcomer win any battle against him.

Within seconds all three dogs were fighting one another, deafening the air with snarls and yelps as teeth bit deep into vulnerable flesh.

Max, used to importunate village dogs, had built her kennel runs strongly, and they were roofed, to prevent an ardent intruder climbing the wire, as one dog had done some years before. The odd-looking pups were sold off at a few pounds each and haunted her by living in the village, reminding her often of something she preferred to forget. The stout door was padlocked and Havoc was safe inside.

Max was as afraid of human thieves after valuable dams and pups, as of importunate suitors for her bitches' favours.

Charlie, hearing the din, raced to sort out the mêlée. The dogs were obsessed and meant to damage one another. This was important to them, and none of them understood that there was no way even the victor could win the lady. She ended the skirmish by throwing a bucket of cold water over them. Spy, soaked and bleeding, separated himself from the others and crept miserably towards Charlie, hoping this human could help him. He had two bad bites, one on his ear and the other on his paw and felt very sorry for himself, once the heat of battle had died in him.

Charlie recognised the dog. She leashed him, and walked him back to Sam's farm.

Sam had finished his evening meal, and was busy with chores that seemed both daunting and endless. From dawn until dark he went from one job to another. He had put his three pigs into a clean sty and was busy mucking out the one they had left. He had not noticed the shed door was open. Trip's door was safely shut.

Susanna, his sow, was due to farrow. He put her in the barn, knowing that his night's rest might well be broken. He would have to check her at midnight; and again at two a.m. She was never a very good mother, and her young might well not be allowed to suck. But her piglets were healthy and grew well, and made good prices when he sold them, and he needed money.

He also needed sleep.

He did not need a soaked dog with a torn ear and badly injured paw that was in obvious need of immediate veterinary attention. He stared at Charlie in dismay.

"How did he get out?" he asked. He walked to the shed and looked at it. The open door told its own tale. He had forgotten the padlock and Spy knew how to shift the latch.

"The sow's due to farrow," he said, hoping that Charlie would understand his worry. She did. She had sat up with too many whelping bitches herself. No good breeder slept when animals were producing young. Too much could go wrong.

Sam looked at Spy. The paw needed stitching, and so probably did the ear. The vet was five miles away, and in that time anything might happen. Sam was torn between two needs. That of his dog and that of his pig.

The opportunity was too good for Charlie to miss.

"Ring the vet and warn him that I'm on my way. I'll take him. He seems to accept me."

"He's a friendly little cuss," Sam said. "Too friendly sometimes; goes to other people when I want to train him."

"He's not friendly with other dogs. He's a fighting demon." Charlie said. "He's bleeding badly. Give me an old towel." Sam stared at her, but did as she asked. He wasn't used to being bossed, but he was grateful for the help offered.

Spy was too unhappy to protest. He suffered the drying towel, and the clean cloth that was bound round his leg, and allowed himself to be led down the road, and put into Charlie's old van. There was a cage at the back for the pups, when she carried them to the vet for inoculations, and Spy went into it meekly and curled up and whimpered softly to himself throughout the journey.

He needed an anaesthetic before either injury could be stitched. Charlie waited. It was almost midnight when she took him home. The light was on in the barn and Sam was busy with his sow.

The shed was cold and the dog needed warmth. Charlie invaded the little farmhouse and found an old blanket flung over a chair. She wrapped the dog up, and left him on the kitchen floor and went back to the barn.

"Three born already," Sam said, exhaustion in his voice and his movements. "She usually has about fifteen."

"Let me stay with her. I'm used to midwifing. Go and get some sleep. I've wrapped your dog up and left him on the kitchen floor. He's had an anaesthetic. And you're going to need some of those piglets to pay the vet bill."

"What about your sleep?"

"I can sleep in the morning. Just let me ring Mum. I don't want her to worry. She said she'd sit up till I got back from the vet's. And if the sow hasn't finished by morning I can stay with her while you're over at Tom's place."

Sam knew that Charlie had a way with beasts; it was the talk of the village. The old men who met nightly in the Black Swan spoke of her with respect in their voices. They told and re-told the tale of how she'd gentled the old bull when he was in a tantrum; and how she had a way with even the wildest dogs. She had a way with horses.

Her grandfather had been a whisperer, they said, a man who could do anything with a horse, and who was called in when everybody else had failed. He'd been a first-class dogman too; won for years at all the local trials and was still talked of with respect although he had been dead for some years.

"No one like old Jacko Hudson."

He had been Max's father.

Charlie had a knack of being at home anywhere and with anyone. She settled in the barn on a bale of straw, ready to intervene if she were needed.

She was not needed. The sow produced twelve more little pigs without any complications. By the time the litter was complete, and the new babies all suckling, dawn had come.

Charlie went into the house. She put fuel into the still-warm Aga, found bacon in the refrigerator and brown eggs in a basket on the old Welsh dresser, where light glinted on faded blue and white Willow pattern plates, made long before she was born.

Sam, waking, still weary, came down the steep winding stairs into his kitchen and stared at her. Spy, aching and stiff, wagged a forlorn tail slightly from side to side.

"I thought you wouldn't mind," Charlie said, laughing

at Sam's astounded expression. "Midwifery makes me hungry and you need food too. Here. Get that inside you."

She pushed a plate full of grilled bacon, fried eggs, fried bread and tomatoes at him. Sam, who normally wolfed down a couple of slices of thick toast and drank a cup of scalding instant coffee before racing off, stared at the food, his mouth watering.

"I'll come and help you with Tom's farm," Charlie said. "You can't go on doing two men's work for ever. I've time on my hands and I'm used to sheep ... and sheepdogs," she added. "I'll see to Spy; and make sure those bites are healing properly, and then bring him over, if that's what you do with him."

The words tumbled out of her. There was so much to do, so much to be said, so little time always. Sam, much slower of thought, was bemused. Charlie had introduced two new ideas at once into his head and he didn't know which to cope with first.

"Why should you help with Tom?"

"Why not? "Charlie asked. She couldn't think of a dafter question. "Why do you? Just as a good neighbour. Why shouldn't I be a good neighbour too? Do you want Spy brought over or not?"

"He's no use," Sam said. "It doesn't matter whether he comes or not. He'll never make a sheepdog."

"He's not much more than eight months old; four and a half years old in human terms. How much do you ever teach a human child of that age?" Charlie was suddenly so angry that she stopped eating, and jabbed her fork at Sam. "You teach it manners and to be sensible, and try to teach it not to dash across the road or tease the cat. You don't teach it to drive. That's what you're trying to do with Spy. He needs to learn slowly; he can't learn all at once and you're muddling him."

Charlie had jumped in with both feet. Sam swallowed, and was about to reply when she plunged on, determined somehow to make this stupid male see her point. "The dog's a sensitive creature; you frighten him. You tell him one thing with your voice, another with your body and a third with your hands. Your hands fly all over the place and collies are hand-sensitive. Look, let me help you with the dog ... my grandfather taught me well. And so did my mother. You've no one to help. Tom's forgotten too much; he works by instinct now but he can't pass on what he's learned; he's too old, too tired, too occupied with keeping himself on his feet when he ought to be resting."

The food was too good to waste. It was hard to be angry with Charlie who had no idea she was giving offence. Sam hardly knew her; had been aware of her, had rarely spoken to her and here she was sitting in his home, cooking on his stove, using his food and laying down the law as if she had lived there all her life and had known him for ever.

"You have to think like a dog," Charlie said. "Spy's young; he can't learn to herd in a moment; can't behave with wisdom when he wasn't born thirty-two weeks ago; he needs time. Time to grow up; time to learn to respect you, to adore you, to behave as if you were his god. At present you're just the man he lives with; a man who he can't understand; a man who isn't predictable at all. Sometimes angry with him but he never knows why; and do you ever praise him, tell him he's done well, make a fuss of him for being a dog, and a lovely animal to have around? Or are you always too busy to care, asking the impossible, wanting him to grow up before he's had a chance?"

Spy, hearing his name, was watching them intently. His

sensitive ears, which were pricked halfway, but flopped at the top, moved gently backwards and forwards as if he were following every word.

Sam began to think. An eight-month pup; and Mel was four years old. Four years of herding, of training, of working with the sheep.

"Spy has to learn sheep; he's born knowing some of it all but not all of it. He has to know how to cope with a stroppy ewe with a new lamb, in need of help. He has to learn how to handle a flock that has never known a dog before and that rushes and bounces and challenges his authority. He has to learn how to cope with pet ewes that are always uppity with the dogs; with the timid ewe that runs from him, desperate to get away; with sheep with the wind under their tails, half mad with recklessness when the gale is blowing, never seeing sense, driving even an experienced dog wild. He has to learn patience; he has to learn control; he has to learn that he can't chase rabbits when he is herding sheep. He's only an animal; not a human in a fur coat. You have to teach him. He can't do it alone."

Sam mopped the egg yolk from his plate with a thick hunk of bread, and chewed thoroughly before he spoke. Charlie's mind seemed to run like quicksilver, and he couldn't keep up with her. He was bewildered by her vehemence and by the new thoughts she was putting into his head. He never had thought about the sheep as characters, or about the dog as being new to the ways of the world.

"He was terrified by the thunder," Sam said. He hadn't recognised it until then as terror; merely as disobedience. Charlie taught without knowing that she did so.

"Havoc was too," Charlie said. "But she's learned it can't hurt her and she manages to cope though she trembles while she's working if we have to work in a storm. She's a brave little bitch."

Sam cut himself a hunk of bread, spread it thickly with butter and ladled on marmalade. Charlie, more dainty, made herself a thin slice of toast. She chewed, and then suddenly looked at Sam and laughed.

"I'm sorry," she said. "Invading your home, cooking your food and eating it, and then lecturing you. It isn't fair. Mum says I'm like a bulldozer, and about as tactful. Only I do care so much about the dogs, and so many people just don't give them a chance. They get angry and that frightens the poor animal, and once they're scared, they stop trying to work. Imagine a giant roaring at you all the time; yelling at you and telling you everything you do is wrong. That's how so many people treat their dogs. Stupid dog, they say. It isn't the dog that's stupid; it's just an animal ... it's the stupid owner who won't take the trouble to understand what's happening inside his dog's head."

"I never thought about it from his viewpoint," Sam said. He glanced at the clock. "Tom will be needing me. You ought to go and get some sleep."

He hesitated.

"Thank you for sitting up with the sow; and for my breakfast."

Thanks didn't come easily to Sam. Few people had ever bothered to help him before and none since he moved to the valley.

Charlie was impatient.

"I can go to bed early tonight. You're sleepwalking; and Tom is barely able to stand up. That arthritis of his is getting worse."

Charlie knew, only too well, that arthritis was always a hazard for a farmer. Heavy loads and long hours labouring in the wet caused aching muscles and creaking joints.

"Oh yes, I know it's none of my business and I'm interfering but dear heaven, man, you need help, both of you and if you're too proud to take it Tom will be dead and you selling your farm as you won't be able to keep it going. I do have eyes in my head; and I do live just down the road and I can't help understanding what I see."

Sam felt he was being swept away by the tide, was being carried out to sea, and was sinking, not even trying to swim. Charlie only came up to his shoulder; he had to look down at her, yet she filled the room with her energy, bursting with her need to make him understand her viewpoint. He did not realise the two men had been in her thoughts for months and that she had worried about them, seeing what was happening to them day by day, longing to help, yet not knowing how to introduce herself.

Now she had an opportunity and did not intend to let it slip.

Sam locked the door behind him. Spy had followed them out, limping badly on his stitched paw. Charlie took him into his shed and as the old Land Rover coughed its way out of the yard, she knelt by the little dog. He was sore and aching and miserable and crept across the straw. She held out her arms to cuddle him.

Nobody had ever cuddled him. The two men rewarded him occasionally with a pat. Sam, sometimes, impatient, lifted him and carried him, but never with real affection.

The little dog longed for comforting hands on his body and somebody to approve of him. He crept into her lap and leaned against her shoulder, and whimpered. She sat there for a long time, and then took the bowl of food that Sam had given her and watched the pup eat.

At least his injuries hadn't affected his appetite. She closed the door on him and went into the next shed with

Trip's food. Even Sam knew it wasn't wise to leave the two dogs together. They had never liked one another. The older collie greeted her with enthusiasm, tired of being alone. His white-tipped tail waved and his black chunky body wriggled with delight.

She watched him race around the farmyard, his nose busy, enquiring into the events of the previous evening. He sniffed at the blood trail left by Spy; at a scatter of straw, where a hen had crouched the evening before; at the edge of the old bath that served to keep water for the animals. The fox had drunk from that, standing on his hind paws to reach. Trip investigated thoroughly, cocked his leg and ran off to herd the ducks.

Charlie whistled to him. He had no desire to come, but there was something in her voice that made him stop and consider her. An authority that his master lacked. He recognised it and obeyed it.

He went quietly to his shed, and the door was shut again. The dog spent too much time locked up and she intended to change that but better to make haste slowly. She had already said much more than she intended.

"The fool that jumps in where angels fear to tread," her mother often said, exasperated by her daughter's impetuous ways. "You never learn, Charlie."

She did learn, but what she learned was not always what Max expected to her learn. Her daughter was sometimes as difficult to understand as her husband had been.

Charlie recognised that Sam was like a stubborn dog, unwilling to accept any authority but his own, unwilling to change his ways, unwilling to believe he could be wrong.

She had maybe made matters much worse; and when he had time to think he would chase her out of his life with anger. It had been hard for him to do that when she had cooked him a meal and sat with his sow. He felt the need to be grateful; but gratitude might not help her at all.

She put Spy into her van, and drove back to the kennels, where her mother looked at her, and saw from her expression that there was something wrong.

"Said more than you meant; told him off. That temper of yours will make for trouble, my girl."

Max knew her daughter very well.

"I'm going to help them," Charlie said. "It's crazy for one man to do so much. He's killing himself."

A few minutes for a quick bath and to change her clothes and then she was off again. Max watched the van drive away. Charlie ran after some wild hares at times, but this was the wildest yet. Max wondered what was motivating her daughter, who had had little time for men in her life so far.

But Charlie had no time to consider her motives. She only knew there was a job to be done and she could do it. She could give Tom a chance to rest and regain his strength. If he had a chance to ease up on the work, his protesting body might heal itself, and he would regain his strength.

Whether the men wanted her or not, she was going to help them.

TEN

CHARLIE's van rattled into the yard. Tom was feeding the chickens, propping himself against the farmhouse wall, looking as if he were too weary to move again. His face was grey, and his dark eyes sunk in deep shadows.

He was irritated with himself. The pains in his hip and knees and hands seemed to dominate him. They also infuriated him. He wasn't all that old. But rheumatism nagged at a man, taking his energy, dulling his wits, slowing his limbs. He wanted to run as fast as Sam, to work with the dogs again, to compete in the trials again.

That was something he would not do now. Never be able to walk the course, or stand for the length of time required, or be quick enough with his commands to his dog. Not for competition.

There were compensations. Days when the sun shone brightly and the pain eased, and his farm creatures made him laugh. Today the chickens dived and darted and pecked at one another, fighting for the grain.

Sam, looking hard at the old man for the first time, felt shock and anger at himself. He ought to have noticed. It had needed this wretched girl to point out to him that the old man was ill.

Tom turned his head slowly and stared at the intruder. Her van had backfired as she cut the engine, and Mel was barking. Bessie joined in, hoping the newcomer meant food.

"I took Spy to the vet for Sam last night," Charlie said. "He's out of action and in need of nursing . . . and I thought you could do with some help. My mother doesn't need me; she can manage on her own these days."

Sam stared at her. Her voice had sounded forlorn. Almost a plea for something to do; a girl with time on her hands, and nothing to fill the long days. None of the firm confidence with which she had greeted him.

Charlie was determined that Tom should accept her and that she didn't upset him. "Normally I'd train Havoc; you know how well she's doing in trials. But she's in season. I've three weeks on my hands. Please let me help. I can do anything on the farm or in the house and I expect you'd like meals cooked for you for a change, while you and Sam are busy."

She turned towards the house, as if expecting to be invited in.

"I'm not looking for a paid job . . . just something to do. And I am good with animals."

"Jacko's granddaughter," Tom said, placing her at last.

"That was a long time ago. Never can remember his name; or your dad's."

Tom had a brief flash of memory; himself with a brave black and white dog with a rakish face. Old Nim ... a rare dog at the Trials, and many a crook they'd won at the local shows. Jacko had his best dog, a veteran named ... the name had gone, but Tom could see the dog. They'd been lying neck and neck, mark for mark the same, and at the end of it Nim had that one extra point that made all the difference.

He and Jacko had shaken hands and drunk their dogs' health that evening and re-lived every moment, going over every inch of the course. The fetch and the lift, and the drive, and the shedding; that was where Nim had triumphed. Jacko had one sheep break away at the last minute.

"Jacko Hudson." Charlie was looking about her, at the cobbled yard, the pecking hens, ranging free, the old sheep baaing her head off, and Mel, now settled at her master's feet, eyeing her with wary interest. "And I'm Charlie Leigh."

"Jacko was a good friend," Tom said. He led the way into the kitchen, across the puddled yard. Charlie looked at the place in dismay. The roof needed mending; the yard needed re-making. The cobbles were so worn that in winter they would be lethal. Tom might so easily break his hip, falling.

Mud where the pond had overflowed. Mel lay at the door, waiting for them. She watched them intently, and lifted her head to sniff the air. Spy was there, but he smelled wrong. She went to the van to investigate, and jumped in. She examined him minutely, wondering at his breath which still retained the taste of anaesthetic, and at the odd smell of his bandaged paw and stitched ear.

She settled beside him, aware he needed comfort, and licked his face.

Sam did not need her as yet, and he left her with the pup, who showed no desire to come out into the yard. His body ached. He was bruised and the two bites hurt. His leg had swollen.

Tom eased himself into the big wicker chair by the fire. Coal burned bravely, blue, yellow and red flames dancing. Tom had dusted and washed the dishes but the place needed brightening up. New curtains and new covers for the cushions would make a world of difference.

"Rest today," Charlie said. "Let me take over for a bit; you're tired."

Tom looked at her. A merry lass, with Jacko's way with beasts and her father's red hair and tremendous energy. He remembered Harry Leigh now. A man with a ready laugh, that boomed unexpectedly. A man who took life lightly, yet always had a word for the lonely, and a sympathy for those in need.

A shame he had to die young.

Charlie was busy sweeping the hearth. She couldn't bear untidiness.

Sam watched her. She worked here, as she had in his home, as if she belonged. It was impossible to resent her. She was already at the sink, filling the kettle. Putting it to boil, pouring hot water into the coffee mugs, each ornamented with a painted bull. A Jersey, a Shorthorn, a Friesian.

Sam went out into the yard. Tom sat, savouring the warmth, aware of the burden of his aching body, of his need to rest. If only his sons had not emigrated; if only he had a granddaughter near, like this. Lucky Jacko. Unlucky Jacko who hadn't lived to enjoy her.

Charlie covered the old man with a rug. He chuckled

to himself. He must seem as old as the standing stone in the churchyard to her, but he wasn't that old. Even so, he was grateful for the extra warmth, and soon was sound asleep.

There were always things to do in a house and the men had been too busy to bother about the finer details. She swept and cleaned and shone the windows. She took the dusty plates from the old dresser, and returned them, gleaming. She polished the brass candlesticks on the mantelpiece and the silver frame around the wedding picture of Tom and his wife, taken nearly fifty years ago, she guessed.

A girl no older than Charlie, wearing a quaint dress; the flowered veil framing a dark-eyed face that laughed up at a sturdy young man, taller than his bride by over twelve inches. Tom was stooped now; only his eyes were the same.

Charlie found bacon and eggs and potatoes. Half an hour later she woke Tom and called Sam in. The two men stared at the table. Neither had ever bothered with a cloth before and Tom wondered where she had found it.

A bright red and white check. Plates of grilled bacon and fried potato cakes, and baked beans. Usually the two men stopped briefly for a drink of tea and thick sandwiches of bread and cheese. There was never time for either to cook a meal.

Charlie, watching the men eat, saw colour come to Sam's face, and a smile to Tom's.

"Ee lass, this is good," the old man said. "If you've really nowt to do, then come by all means and welcome; we need a woman round here. I've not had a meal to touch this since Mary died."

"I've cleaned up for you. There are clean sheets on your bed; and I've washed everything I could find that needed it." Charlie had been thankful that the farm boasted a modern washing machine. The curtains needed to be done too; and the bedding. Time enough. She'd a job for life here.

The men had kept the place tidy, but there was neither comfort nor luxury. The shabby rooms needed re-decorating and there was a lot of outdoor maintenance left undone. She could do some of that. She was handy with a saw, and a chisel and a plane. She could also mend the fences. Goodness knew why the lambs weren't all over the village. The place was falling apart.

Max had never had enough money to cover the constant repair of the kennels. Both women had had to learn how to manage without a man.

A reluctant sun, hiding among moving clouds, warmed the air. Sam was busy with the sheep, using Mel, who worked for him unwillingly, and not always with obedience. She and Tom were a team. She endured Sam, who was never fast enough to anticipate her needs, so that often she drove the sheep without commands, bringing them to him so that he could inspect them for signs of ill health.

Charlie, watching, longed to take over, but knew it would not be wise. She had said enough already. Maybe too much. Though Tom accepted her happily, Sam was wary, looking for motives, distrusting her. She lifted Spy from the van, and took him into the little enclosure behind the farm, a high-walled yard where the bitches were put when in season.

She couldn't bear to see a badly trained dog. She was sure the dog could be taught well; perhaps to trials standard one day, but that day was in the future. He had to walk before he could run. Had to learn that humans were to be obeyed, and that he must wait for their commands, not hasten to obey his own instincts, which, at his age, could lead him astray.

She had watched him often enough with Sam to know he was far too eager to herd his sheep. That had to be curbed. She put a pen in the yard; four hurdles, locked together. She went into the barn where she knew the ram was kept. She led him, protesting, using a head collar, and put him in the pen.

Spy was sore, and not inclined to riot. It was a good time to start a lesson. Not too long; the dog was far from fit. His keenness was an asset, but it had to be cured. The smell of the sheep overcame his misery; he forgot his sore paw and ear, and crept forward.

He circled the pen, the ram watching him suspiciously. It put its head down, annoyed at this brash youngster. Spy, forgetting his injuries, flew at the metal bars and tried to nip. The ram charged. The hurdles held him, and he shook his head angrily.

Charlie always had a light line in her pocket with a clip at the end of it. She had put a collar on Spy the night before, to attach a lead to him. She knew from the way he behaved that walks on a lead had never been a major part of his life. He had pulled relentlessly, determined to get away from her and the restriction round his throat.

In the end she carried him. An injured dog, suffering from shock, could not be taught anything.

Charlie whistled; the whistle that all the shepherds used to tell the dog to go down, to watch the sheep, not to move until a further command was given. Spy dropped, but as the ram shifted in the pen, the dog flew at him again.

The tug on the cord checked him, together with the sharp whistle.

Charlie's hand was firm on his shoulders, she was holding him down, willing him to stay there, not to move, not to jump up and rush in. Spy had to learn that a dog must obey, especially if he were a sheepdog.

The pup had not learned he should not rush at sheep; Sam had never been able to cure him and the fault had grown. The smallest movement from the ram triggered the dog. "Lie still, Spy. Lie still. Don't dare move." Her voice was soft but commanding, with no hint of anger. Nothing to trigger fear. Charlie was faster than Sam. Charlie was firmer than Sam, and she was not going to let the pup disobey her.

The lesson lasted for just over half an hour. During it, Spy learned a number of new things. He learned there were humans who were more determined than he was. He learned that, with Charlie, he had to do as he was told. And he also learned that if he did not come to her the moment she said come, the lead at his throat snatched at him, and brought him, in spite of himself, in response.

There was a lot of work to do. She had to undo months of free running; months of little training, months during which a headstrong pup had become more headstrong.

Also he had to learn again which signals were given. Sam had confused him. Charlie gave him the same signal every time. Lie down, pup. Lie down, pup. Over and over, until he realised that that noise and that movement told him what to do.

And that when he pleased her he was praised extravagantly. He had never been praised before when he did right.

Good boy, clever boy, the soft voice sang at him, delight in its tone. Delight that told him he was doing well for this woman who had taken him in hand; delight that told him he was a good dog, when he did as he was asked.

At the end of half an hour he understood he was not allowed to move until Charlie gave him another cue. Not even if the ram were enticing him, not even if the sheep smell were maddening him, making him want to fly at the pen, to hold the ram with all his strength, as a sheepdog should. He also learned that the second she said "come" he had to come. When he came to her for the fifth time, without delay, she hugged him and he snuggled against her.

Lessons with Charlie, he discovered, were fun. She did not get angry with him; she did not move her hands all over the place so that he had no idea what was expected of him. She was easy to understand. He did not even realise he had had a lesson.

Charlie returned the ram to the barn and put the dog in her van again to rest. Little and often, her grandfather had always said, and when the lesson sinks in, let him lie by himself and digest it.

She did not tell Sam that she had been training his dog, and she hoped that old Tom had not seen her.

When Sam went back to his own farm, she stayed on, building the fire, putting a stone hot water bottle in the bed to air it, and cooking a big meat pie that would make several meals. Tom invited her to stay and eat with him. He lacked company and it was a long time since he had anyone other than Sam to talk to. She rang her mother.

Tom had gone to lock the chickens up for the night, and was out of hearing.

"They never eat properly during the day," Charlie said. "Bread and marge and cheese, eaten on the move. I don't know if they have a decent cooked meal at night either. With proper food and rest, he'll be a new man. He's asked me to stay to supper with him."

"Tom? Or Sam?" Max asked.

"I'm talking about the old man," Charlie said.

"Good luck to you, girl." There was laughter in Max's

voice. "Men on their own are pretty hopeless. Women are lucky; we can do their work; they rarely can do ours well. What about the pup?"

"Sam left him with me. He's lost heart and lost interest in training his pup, but he's a good keen dog; and that's the problem. Too lively for a novice."

"Don't you go getting above yourself, my girl," Max said. "That pup might just prove your undoing too. He's wayward; you can see it in his eyes."

Charlie grinned to herself as she rang off. She'd prove them all wrong. Spy was a great pup and had the makings of a great dog. She'd never been wrong yet.

She didn't remember that her mother had never been wrong either and that this was the first time they had disagreed about a dog.

ELEVEN

THE WEEKS passed so fast that Charlie was sometimes breathless. There was so much to do. Work at home, work with her own dog; work with Spy, who relied more and more on her and less and less on Sam.

Charlie and Max were used to treating elderly dogs suffering from arthritis. Warmth. Max had an infra-red lamp, that eased Tom's pain, so that he slept. There were herbal drinks that Max's own mother had made; and Rhus Tox, that helped their old animals.

Green vegetables; less red meat. Tom laughed at her, but had to admit after some weeks that something was working. Maybe time and rest. Maybe her remedies. Sam was more sceptical. He didn't believe in country medicine.

The district nurse had suggested Charlie made Tom take a course of multi-vitamins. He was moving around the farm again, enjoying his beasts again, and most of all enjoying Charlie, who made him laugh.

Sam was a sober man, with a quick anger that he found hard to hide.

He was jealous, not only of the way that Charlie could handle the dogs, but of her growing influence over Tom. He snapped at both of them. Although he continued to come and do the heavy work, he made an excuse to leave early and not share the evening meal.

Spy was learning. Even Sam had to admit that. He was not a steady dog, but he did now try to keep his speed down, he did try not to hassle the sheep into a wild romp to their destination, and he had learned never to nip. Charlie sent Havoc out to nip him when he nipped the sheep. That taught Spy very quickly.

The dog was now a year old.

Spring turned to summer. The lambs were sold. Haytime came, then harvest. Autumn arrived suddenly with a nip in the air and bright mornings when mist hung over the river valley and the sun glittered through a gilded haze.

Dish and Havoc both had silver cups to show for their prowess during the summer months. A small local sheepdog trial was due to be run.

"Enter Spy," Charlie suggested.

Sam had lost all confidence, and was not sure that he even liked his dog or wanted his dog. Spy ran to greet Charlie when she came in a way that he never greeted his owner. Spy responded fast to her voice, reluctantly to Sam's.

Charlie could play the fool with the dog, entice him to play, and then calm him with a swift signal. If Sam played the dog became unruly, out of hand, showing a wildness that he never developed with Charlie.

Most of all Sam resented Charlie because she was female. It was not right that a woman should be able to best a man. Sam, with a mother who waited on her menfolk, and two sisters encouraged to do the same, saw no reason why a man should perform household chores if a woman were there.

Tom, now feeling ten years younger, enjoying his life again, watched, but said nothing. They had to go their own way, had to learn as he had had to learn. Though sometimes he wondered if Sam could learn. For a young man, his thoughts and attitudes were surprisingly rigid.

At home, in the evenings that he could now enjoy as he was less tired, Sam had to admit to himself that Charlie's help had made an enormous difference. He was not going to admit it to her.

His parents had not believed in praising a child. Gave it a swelled head. Boys did not get kisses or cuddles either. "Be a man," they said, even when he was a tiny boy. Sam gave credit grudgingly, his own confidence having been badly harmed when he was young.

Charlie entered Spy in the trials, with herself as his handler, overruling Sam, who had no choice but to let his dog compete or look a fool. The whole village was now intrigued by the situation up at Tom's place. They thought about it and talked about it, and knew that if Spy were to win the trial, Sam would resent the win.

It was an easy course designed for young dogs. The first few to run did well, but Charlie knew that Spy could do better. Sam found himself wishing passionately that the dog would make a fool of her. He was sure that if she won she would boast of her skill, and belittle his. He was too absorbed in his own jealousy to realise that

Charlie had never once bragged, and had done her best to interest him in the skill of training.

Tom longed to shake him.

It was a grey day with mist in the air. There was sun behind the mist, patching the hills with light. The field was packed with spectators, all eager to watch the fun, all self-styled experts making wise comments, some of which made Charlie grin to herself as she waited. These were the visitors, pretending to be knowledgeable.

There was an ache in her throat and she wished she had not eaten at lunchtime. Spy mattered more than Havoc though she couldn't say why. Maybe she was confident with Havoc, but with this dog she had a point to prove.

Spy had worked the course before, on the farm. Charlie knew how it would be set, and had laid it out for him. He had worked well then, but this was different. There was nervousness in the air, stemming from other competitors, affecting their dogs. There was her own uneasiness, and doubt. With Havoc she was set to win. She had never before tried with a dog she had not trained from puppyhood, and had not handled every day of its life.

Max had tried to stop her entering.

"He isn't your dog. He could let you down; and then you'll get the blame," Max said.

Tom, watching every movement, found that he was torn between his two friends. If Charlie won with Spy he was sure that Sam would desert him; and if she didn't win her confidence would take a deadly shock.

Though maybe it did people as much good to lose as to win. What had Charlie's grandfather said so long ago? "It's not so much the winning. It's how you play the game."

Those who never failed missed invaluable lessons. Tom chewed at the stem of the pipe that Charlie had persuaded him to stop smoking. He nodded as the dog under test shed its sheep neatly and then penned them. Full marks, though he had lost marks on the fetch and the drive.

And now it was Charlie and Spy.

The course looked enormous. Charlie sent her dog and he raced off, looking for his sheep. It was minutes before he found them, as the wind was blowing the wrong way, and he had to search instead of relying on his nose. As soon as he was beyond them he caught the scent and homed in.

It should then have been easy, but luck was against them. Charlie's heart almost stopped. They had chanced on the rogues of the day. The lead sheep, head down, faced the dog, and stamped.

Spy tried to move it, and failed. This was an old ewe, wily and experienced and she knew dogs. She had been hand reared and bottle fed, and was afraid of nothing. Certainly not a youngster that was less than a quarter of her age. She snorted, and butted the dog.

Spy backed off, staring at her in astonishment and then tried to outface her with his eyes. She had no intention of obeying his will. He turned away, asking for a command. Any command. He had no idea what to do.

Charlie whistled and the dog crept round, trying to come behind the ewe. She jumped over him. The other three sheep scattered and ran in different directions. Spy never had a chance, and, faced with mutiny, he lost his head.

He was deaf to every whistle. He chased uselessly, bringing now three sheep together, and now only two. The sheep broke away from him, again and again.

Time was up. One of the older dogs was sent in to round the dodging animals. Even he had a task, but wisdom and experience came to his aid. Charlie whistled to Spy. He came unwillingly, aware of the tenseness of her body, and of her disappointment.

"Bad luck, lass," one of the older men said. "Not had sheep like those before, have you?"

Charlie shook her head, not trusting her voice.

Tom gripped her shoulder.

"No one wins all the time," he said. "The dog had no chance. Pity it was his first trial. It won't help. May destroy his confidence altogether, and make him sheep wary."

That didn't help either.

Sam had hoped that Charlie might be placed, but not win. Oddly, her failure had boosted his own confidence. It wasn't entirely due to his handling that Spy was so difficult. The dog had a mind of his own.

"Rough luck, Charlie," Sam said, as she came towards him. He would have said more, but there was a sudden interruption.

None of them had noticed the small Jack Russell that crept up to Spy, inquisitive. Charlie had not leashed him. He lay at her feet watching the three humans. They were the important people in his life, his family, and he sensed their disappointment.

He had had a bad half hour and Charlie's edginess had communicated itself to him. He curled a lip at the Jackie, and snarled. The Jackie, a seasoned warrior, a nine-to-five dog from the nearby housing estate, bit the sheepdog on the nose.

No sane dog was going to suffer such an indignity. Spy leaped up, chasing the Jackie, who was suddenly afraid. This dog was no easy victim, as other dogs were. Spy reached him, and caught him, and war began.

Two shepherds sprang in, one of them throwing his macintosh over the fighting dogs. Bewildered, and in the dark, they broke off, trying to free themselves from the clinging stinking folds.

Charlie reached Spy, put the cord round his neck, and led him off, aware of eyes behind her, of voices criticising softly, of a dog that was not under full control. A dog that loved to fight. If he were herding sheep and another dog came by, she was sure that Spy would leave his post and attack.

"That fight with Heinie when he was young," Tom said. "Marred him for ever. It often does. That age, they remember. A few weeks earlier, or a few weeks later, it might not have had so much effect. Or it might. Never can tell. Not with dogs."

It was small consolation.

It was a silent party that drove home, the dogs lying in the back of the Land Rover. Spy soon forgot his disastrous afternoon. Only humans brooded. He was exhausted and slept. He ate, and went to his shed. Sam had no desire to keep this dog in the house. He knew nothing but disappointment. Before he closed and padlocked the door, he looked at his collie. He was a handsome fellow. And that was all.

The dog was useless and he needed a decent sheepdog. Maybe he could afford one someone else had trained and learn by working that. Not even Charlie could train Spy.

Sam hadn't time for three dogs. Trip was bad enough, but he did work after a fashion. Spy appeared to have no sense in his small body and to be unable to learn.

One of the men watching that afternoon, behind Sam, had commented with disgust in his voice.

"Did you ever see such a no-good pup?"

The tone and the words had bitten deep into Sam's mind.

Spy would have to go.

TWELVE

OCTOBER was a savage month. Gale succeeded gale. Each tore trees from the ground. Rain flooded the fields. A rockfall altered the shape of the mountain, bringing fear. Further falls might tumble the scree and damage the houses that clung to the slopes.

Tom slipped on the muddy cobbles and sprained his ankle, so he was unable to move far from his chair. He hobbled round the yard, using a stick, and did what he could, but all the heavy work fell on Sam and Charlie.

Two village dogs broke into Sam's sheep field. He found his young ram lamb, of which he had high hopes, torn horribly and screaming with pain. It took an hour for the vet to arrive. He swore profusely and ended the animal's agony.

Nobody had seen the dogs. Two shapes were glimpsed, running down the street, both blood-covered. One woman tried to catch them but the dogs were half crazy with the killing lust, and easily escaped.

There was no compensation for the four hundred pounds that Sam had lost. He couldn't afford to insure every beast on his farm. No farmer could.

No compensation for the shows he might have won; the ewes that could have been put in lamb, to bring out stock as good as the sire. It had been a magnificent beast, the best Sam had ever owned, and he had treasured it, not only for its pedigree, but for its affectionate ways and small amusing habits.

Sam was angry. Whenever he was out in the fields, he carried his gun. No dog would do such damage again. He would shoot as soon as he saw one anywhere near his sheep. And he would encourage Spy to attack the animal and make it suffer as the ram had suffered.

Spy was still with Sam. The dog was endured but not loved. Sam's temper was always near the surface, easily roused, and the collie began to fear his master, which added to the problems.

Spy would always come to Charlie when she called him. He often refused to come to Sam, and when he did, approached head down, tail tucked beneath him, worry in his eyes. He would not approach the man's hands. He stood well back, muscles taut, eyes wary.

Sam's anger tensed his body and tightened his mouth and gave a glare to his eyes. Without realising, the man stared his dog down, terrifying him. Most of the rage was due to the dogs that had killed his best ram, but Spy did not know that. He thought all the temper was directed at him.

Sam joked with Tom and Charlie, and tried to hide his feelings but he could never hide them from his dog. Nor, through the dog's behaviour, could he hide them from Charlie.

Charlie dared not say anything. Sam's tongue lashed her at times, wounding terribly. He sometimes lashed Tom. Then the quick flare of fury would be over, and he would laugh with them. The memory of the ram faded, but Spy was with him still, reminding Sam of failure.

Sam did not like failure.

The girl refused to leave. Tom needed her more than ever now, with Sam so difficult to handle.

Max, watching her daughter, knew that she was unhappy. She was thinner, and her eyes were ringed with darkness. She had lost her quick laugh and her ready retorts, and said little when at home.

Max held her tongue. No one else could live Charlie's life for her. Maybe it had been very unwise to try to help the two men. No point in reminding her daughter of that now.

"The weather can't get worse," the old men said, as they sat and drank their ale in the Black Swan.

They were wrong.

The end of October brought snow, flying in great flakes from a sullen sky hanging low on the mountains, hiding the peaks. Tom, weather-wise, asked Charlie, the night before the storm, to bring in the sheep. Sam stared at him. Blizzards in October? The old man was wandering in his wits.

Sam woke to a world that had changed overnight. Peak and slope, scree and high cliffs were all gone, hidden in a soft covering that lay deep. The cottage walls glowed with faint light. The sky promised more snow to come.

The glisten on the ground was a fantasy, the white boughs and the soft sheen, magical. The beauty was lost on a man who had sheep on the hills.

Sam cursed as he dressed. He should have listened to the old man. Should have known better. If only he had listened. But that didn't mend matters, and there was work to do. He doubted if he could bring the sheep down now. But he would have to find them. Have to try. There would be no time to help Tom today. At least his sheep were in, not separated from him by acres of snow-covered fields.

Sam's own flock had grown and his own farm came first. Charlie would have to help the old man.

Sam floundered as he stepped into his yard. The snow was knee deep, and clung wetly to his legs. No time for food. He dug a channel to Spy's shed and brought the dog out. No use taking Trip in weather like this. The older dog was snow-crazy, flying into the drifts, rolling and butting at the soft surface that triggered him to puppy lunacy. His busy paws flung the glittering flakes into the air.

If only he had a decent dog.

Spy nosed the snow suspiciously. He had forgotten winter. He tasted the cold wetness, and sat in it, surprised to find that it was so deep. He looked at Sam, asking for a command, but Sam only whistled to him to follow, and struggled across the yard to the far gate.

The first flakes of the day drifted on the needling wind, clinging to the dog's fur and the man's clothing. Spy shook them off impatient but as fast as he shook himself, more settled.

Sam would have to find his sheep, have to try to bring them near to the house, as they would need feeding with hay and there was no way to take it across the fields and over the stile. Nor could he get round by road with the tractor. The mountain slip had completely blocked the old lane.

The weather was an enemy, determined to defeat him. The gate fought him, snow lying deep against it. He slipped into the ditch, falling headlong. Swearing, he dragged himself out.

He hated the world, and he hated the farm, and he hated the sheep and he loathed his dog.

He even hated Charlie.

He was not going to be beaten by the storm.

Spy, his legs almost hidden by the snow, jumped himself along. They left scored marks behind them. The dog's body dragged a furrowed ridge and deep holes showed where Sam had trodden.

Spy watched his pluming breath, puzzled.

The sheep were against the hedge, many of them buried. The dog nosed his way, barking when he found one of the frightened animals. They were too scared to even try to move.

Snow was falling more heavily, the wind behind it. Though early in the morning, the day was midnight dark. The stinging flakes were hail hard. Spy shook himself and shook himself again, and plodded on, his instinct telling him to quarter the ground and bark when he found a sheep. Sam did not realise that the dog was helping him. The man thought the desperate barking was induced by the weather conditions. It was an added irritation.

He did not try to find out whether there was a ewe buried or not. He did not even think of it. Spy became totally frustrated, knowing things the man did not. Knowing also that the sheep needed rescuing. He tried to dig but the drifts against the hedges were deep and the snow he dug away fell back into the holes he made.

Sam was very cold and he was hungry. He had not

dressed warmly. He cursed continuously, blaming all the world for his misfortunes, never blaming himself.

Disaster waited at the far hedge where rocks lay buried, fallen from the hills during the slide. Sam had not seen them, as he had not walked across that particular field. He stepped on to one of the tumbled boulders and it moved.

His leg was trapped.

As he fell, he knew it was broken. He lay, shaking with shock.

Spy nosed him anxiously. Sam could not speak. The pain was too severe. The dog was frantic, aware that something was very wrong. He began to dig at the snow, his busy paws sending the flakes flying.

Sam stared at his leg. He couldn't move it; nor move the great boulders that held him fast. He managed to prop himself against another rock, but there was nothing he could do to free himself.

He tugged at the rocks with both hands. Pain knifed through him, so that he wanted to scream. There was nobody in sight, although he was only four fields from home. Nobody would think of looking for him here. Nobody would come. Nobody else would have been such a fool as to venture out alone, in such weather.

There had been eight deaths on the slopes that year. His cottage was on the flight path for the Mountain Rescue helicopter, and he often heard it drumming through the night. Another victim of the hills. He had read in the morning papers of men and women who had challenged the mountains, been lost in the mist and died of exposure.

Men and women who were uninjured. Cold killed. Respect the sea and respect the high hills, Tom often said. Both demand sacrifices from stupid humans who forget that the mountains are slayers.

Above loomed the high peaks, deep in snow. There could be an avalanche. The boulders had fallen here; the snow could follow. Lying buried, unable to breathe, unable to see....

He was sick with pain. His anorak was not waterproof, nor was it padded, and he was already shivering with cold. If only there were sheep near that would huddle against him, but nothing moved.

Memory betrayed him. He thought of the monument in the Peak District to the little dog that had stayed by his master's dead body until the thaw came, and the shepherd was found. He had only been a short distance from safety. He had wandered in the mist and fallen from exhaustion. Nobody had thought to look for him.

The snow killed. The cold killed. The mountains killed. Black clouds spoke of a blizzard to come. He could be buried in a few hours, and then how would anyone know where to look for him?

The old men were right and he should have listened to them. Too late now to mend his ways. He would never have another chance. If he did. ... He began to pray, though God had never been part of his life. Never again. Never to walk the hills; never to tend the sheep. Never to talk to Tom. Never to train a dog.

Never to see Charlie. Charlie. ... Why had he been so cruel to her? He needed her now. Longed for her to come across the fields, to kneel beside him, to hold his head in her warm hands, to soothe away the pain.

Drifting in and out of consciousness, he began to remember so many things.

Childhood rhymes, from long ago, and simple prayers.

He had memories of kneeling by his bed, his mother sitting above him, her voice soft, encouraging him. If only he were a child again, safe in his bed at home, his parents coming up to tell him a last story before they switched off the light.

They said that all your life floated before you when you were dying. If only someone would come. Why should anyone bother to look for him? If only Charlie were here. Charlie with her quick laugh and her soft touch, and her eyes watching him, sadness in them because he had shouted at her again.

Charlie could do so many things well and he begrudged her her success.

"Please God, let them come," he said to the lowering sky. "Let them find me Charlie, I need you." He shouted her name, as if that would bring her. "Charlie, please come. Charlie, I want you."

He did need her and he had never realised it. And now it was too late.

The snow was covering him slowly, remorselessly. Soon he would be as hidden as his sheep, to lie till the thaw came and men discovered him. They'd bury him in the churchyard where the trees shaded the little graves, and the mountains watched. Would Charlie mourn for him? Would she put flowers on his grave? Speak of him with kindness when he had gone for ever? He didn't want to die. He lay shivering violently, his teeth chattering.

Where was Spy? The beastly dog had deserted him. He might have hugged the animal, taking warmth from the small furry body. Now the little brute had deserted him. He'd get rid of him when he got out of this. Only he never would get out of this.

Sam wanted to live. To make amends. To tell Charlie he loved her. This was a totally unexpected thought and it amazed him. It kept him warm for a few moments. He had to get free.

When he was free he would marry Charlie.

He had to shift the rocks. He tried again, but when he moved the pain returned, preventing any rational thought.

Spy, struggling desperately back through the fields, knew that something was very wrong. His need for help from other humans dragged him through the darkening day, the sky so full of snow clouds that light was only a memory. He was making for the glowing patchwork windows of the village, for the safety of the main street and for Charlie.

Charlie would tell him what to do. He trusted her, as he had never trusted Sam.

It was, at first, easier to return, floundering in the furrows he had made. The new snow was settling by the time he reached the second field. He pushed through the bars of the gate, and into the lane. Here it was easier to trot, as the snow plough had cleared a path and the new fall was only inches deep.

Charlie was feeding her dogs when Spy arrived and barked at her.

"Spy's escaped," she called to her mother. "I'll keep him here. Sam must have gone over early to help Tom."

Spy barked again and again, irritated by her stupidity. He needed her to follow him and she wouldn't listen.

Charlie took another bowl and put food in front of him. The dog barked again, and backed away from her, towards the gate. There was no time to eat. She stared at him. He ran to her and took her wrist in his mouth and tried to drag her, desperate with his need.

Max, who had come into the yard, looked at the dog.

"There's something wrong. Maybe Sam's hurt. I'll get the men from the two farms down the road. We'd better follow the dog."

Charlie waited, impatience mastering her. Hours seemed to pass before the men came, wrapped in thick duffle coats, their heads hidden under thick knitted balaclava helmets, each carrying a blanket.

They knew too much about snow. Snow that hid the beasts. Snow that killed the unwary.

They looked at the dog. They also knew dogs. Spy was dancing with impatience, circling on the spot, running round them, barking at them.

"He wants us to come ... something bad," one of the men said.

Sam's mind wandered in and out of reality, remembering small things that had happened, calling to Charlie to help him, calling on God to take pity on him. Please let me be warm, he said through chattering teeth, feeling the dreadful chill inch through his body. He would never be warm again.

Then pain overcame all other feelings and he drifted in and out of consciousness.

He heard the voices, heard the barking dog, but he was lost in despair, his leg throbbing, sickness blinding him to everything around him. He was numb with cold, drifting away from the world into a merciful unconsciousness from which he roused again to a terrible place in which fear of dying gave way to a longing for rest for ever.

"Hold on, son," a voice said. "We'll have you home and warm in no time."

Hands worked together to release the rock, but Sam did not know that. He had fainted. Charlie knelt beside him, putting over him the warm blankets that the men had brought, lying Spy and Havoc against him, to give him the warmth that his body was losing. He was so cold; cold with the dreadful coldness of imminent death.

"Don't die, Sam," she said to his unheeding ears. "Don't leave me. I need you." That thought surprised her, but she knew, as she held on to him, willing him to live, that she did need him, and always had.

She was alone with him; the men had gone to find more help, to bring a stretcher. They would be too late. She put both dogs on one side of him and lay against him, under the blankets, holding him close, trying to bring warmth back into his body. Havoc licked his face, her maternal instincts telling her this man was in need. There was nothing to do but pray, as the snow fell, covering their bodies. She would die beside him; she and the dogs, all of them sacrificed to this man's stubbornness. No other man would have ventured out alone in such weather.

"Oh Sam, you are such a fool," she said, trying to rub his hands and face warm with her gloved hands, trying to still her own fears.

The men returned from the nearest farm with a door to use as a stretcher. Their heavy feet had beaten a trail through the fields, but the snow was now falling more heavily, covering everything again. It was a race against the weather, and against the dreadful cold that was engulfing Sam.

"No chance of hospital till this lot goes," Joe Gardiner from Hollow Dene Farm said, as he helped Charlie to pile blankets on to the spare bed in her own home. "Maybe the district nurse can get here, and splint that leg and give him something for the pain. Phones are all down, and the doctor's in the next valley."

Men went off to help Tom. Joe collected four other men to take hay to Sam's sheep. Spy settled by his master, his eyes never leaving his face.

He lay there while the district nurse splinted the leg, and gave him an injection to kill the pain. The piled blankets warmed him, and at last Charlie knew she could stop being afraid. He could not have the leg plastered until the snow had gone, but the nurse thought the fracture clean, and there was no danger of any infection. His thick trousers had protected the leg from skin injury.

He would be on crutches for weeks, and he would need her more than ever before. Joe had promised to find men to help Tom. The villagers had not realised how frail the old man had become. Maybe ill winds did blow some good.

Spy only left the bedroom to go out and to feed. He lay there for most of three days, while Sam drifted in and out of consciousness.

The man woke on the third day, clear-headed and hungry, though his leg hurt abominably. When Charlie came in to look at him, Sam stared at her. His face was damp with sweat.

"How did I get here?"

"Spy fetched me. If it hadn't been for him you'd be dead."

Sam looked at his dog. He whistled, and Spy walked, uncertainly, to the bedside. He had been lying on a rug near the door. Sam patted the blanket and the dog leaped up beside him, and cuddled against him, joyously aware of the man's approval of him, of the caressing hand. His tail beat a tattoo on the quilt as he revelled in the soft unusual words of praise.

"Good lad. Clever lad. I misjudged you, didn't I?" Sam said. "I was going to get rid of him. I was wrong about him. He's a terrific dog. When we're married we'll mate him to Havoc and get a litter of pups, and you can teach me how to handle them."

Charlie stared at him, and then she laughed.

"I think you're delirious," she said. "Though come to think of it, marriage sounds like a good idea. You need someone to stop you doing crazy things, like going out in the worst weather we've had for years, without even putting proper clothes on."

It wasn't exactly a romantic proposal or acceptance, but Sam and Charlie were satisfied.

Spy, aware of happiness in the air, wagged his tail at them, and then snuggled up to Sam and licked his face. The man tightened his arms around the dog, holding on to him for comfort in his pain, knowing that never again would he blame an animal for what was a human's fault.

He held out his hand to Charlie, who took it, and held it tight. For both of them, there was to be a new beginning. Spy settled himself so that he could be close to her too, but he did not leave Sam. The man had praised his dog, and Spy knew that from that day on, there would be trust and a bond between them.

The no-good pup had proved his worth.